GEORGE FRIDERIC HANDEL
Composer of *Messiah*

Listening to, or participating in, the singing of Handel's *Messiah* is now as much a part of Christmas celebrations as the buying of gifts. And that experience will be richer yet for people who realize the series of miracles that were required to bring this oratorio into being.

While a lad of seven, Handel's barber-surgeon father assured him that he would rather his son's fingers be cut off than that he become a musician. To emphasize this, he burned all the boy's musical toys in the fireplace. Nonetheless, young George Frideric continued to practice on a muted clavichord hidden in the attic.

Later, Handel had to overcome a paralysis of his right arm. Shortly before working on *Messiah*, he was so pressed for money he feared debtor's prison. Yet Providence brought him to that momentous time in his life. After composing the "Hallelujah Chorus," he exclaimed through tears to a servant, "I did think I did see all heaven before me, and the great God himself!"

At the first London performance of the *Messiah*, King George II rose to his feet during the singing of the "Hallelujah Chorus," and since he was King, the rest of the audience rose with him. Thus began the custom which continues to this day.

Altogether, Handel composed as much music as the combined works of Johann Sebastian Bach and Ludwig Beethoven. And much of his music still lives to glorify the God whom Handel served with his great talent.

ABOUT THE AUTHOR

Charles Ludwig, son of missionaries, grew up in Kenya. He has traveled in scores of countries and preached in many of them. For a number of years he was a pastor and evangelist. He also wrote. His writings include one thousand articles, stories and serials. He has been translated into numerous languages and has published over forty books. In 1979 he received a National Religious Book Award for his book on Michael Faraday.

Author Ludwig especially likes to write biographies. In preparing for this book, he spent time in the museums and libraries of London. He photographed buildings that Handel knew and used, examined Handel's handwritten scores, and read old books about Handel, all so that he could make this biography as accurate as possible. He hopes that young people, and grownups too, will enjoy this story and will come to more fully appreciate the great music Handel has left us.

ABOUT THE ARTIST

Arthur Schneider, who studied children's book illustration at the University of Michigan, has had a long, full, and varied career in art before this book provided him with the moment to achieve that early goal.

"Never be afraid to try something new," he tells young people, and advises them to practice with a goal in mind so that when the opportunity presents itself, they can do it. In art, as in all of life, practice and perserverence are most important. "After all," he says, "the career of the Olympic runner didn't start at the sound of the starter's gun."

George Frideric Handel

Composer of Messiah

T 17677

by

Charles Ludwig

illustrated by **Arthur Schneider**

MOTT MEDIA

For my sister Fern,
the musical genius
of the family

COPYRIGHT © 1987 Mott Media, Inc.

Kurt Dietsch, Cover Artist

LIBRARY OF CONGRESS CATALOGING IN PUBLICATION DATA

Ludwig, Charles, 1918-
    George Frideric Handel: Composer of *Messiah*.

    (The Sowers Series)
    Bibliography: p. 180
    Includes Index.

    SUMMARY: A biography of the composer of more than forty operas, nineteen oratorios, including the famous "Messiah," and hundreds of other vocal and instrumental works.
    1. Handel, George Frideric, 1685-1759–Juvenile literature. 2. Composers–Biography–Juvenile literature. [1. Handel, George Frideric, 1685-1759. 2. Composers] I. Schneider, Arthur, ill. II. Title. III. Series: Sowers.

ML3930.H25L8 1987   780'.92'4 [B] [92]   87-42683
ISBN 0-88062-048-X Paperbound

CONTENTS

EXPLANATORY NOTES

The roots of all George Frideric Handel books extend into the primary works of John Mainwaring, *Memoirs of the Life of the Late George Frideric Handel*, published in London in 1760; and Johann Matterson's book, published in Hamburg in 1739.

Too many books about Handel have concentrated on sifting evidence. Was Handel seven or nine when he caught up with his father's carriage on its way to Weissenfels? Was the libretto for *Messiah* written by Charles Jennens as Handel believed, or his clerical servant Pooley, as some historians believe? Such questions are important. But they are beyond my purpose.

For the sake of the story, I have avoided such arguments. Yet this biography is as close to truth as I can make it. The one completely ficticious character is Petrina, the cat. And the only invented scene is the one in the baths at Aix-la-Chapelle where an anonymous person speaks to Handel.

There are numerous ways of spelling Handel and his given names. I have chosen those most commonly used in the English-speaking world. Handel was fluent in German, French, Italian, and English. But his English was rather broken. I have only had him speak in a broken way when he spoke in English. I have done this in order to avoid monotony.

In places, I have retained Eighteenth-Century English spelling. Thus, I have written *musick* instead of music. Likewise, I have retained most of the punctuation in contemporary quotes.

In some encyclopedias and other publications, Handel's middle name is spelled Frederick. The preferred way among researchers, however, is *Frideric*, and that is the spelling I have used.

Charles Ludwig

1

You Will Be A Lawyer!

As George Handel leaned across the breakfast table, his face was rigid with determination. Glowering at Anna, sitting opposite from him he snapped: "Go up to George Frideric's room and bring down his musical toys. All of them!"

Startled, George Frideric stared. In all his seven years he had never heard such sternness in his father's voice, nor seen such fierceness in his eyes. Framed in white wavy hair that flowed over his shoulders, his father's face had become as determined as an ax.

George Frideric's heart pounded.

"Right now?" inquired the lady he had addressed as Anna.

"Yes, right now!" Handel slapped the table with the palm of his hand.

"B-but the bacon and eggs are already on the table. We'll be late for church."

"That doesn't matter. When a patient of mine has

been bitten by a snake I don't hesitate.'' He glowered at his son. ''George Frideric is growing up. It's my duty to shape his life. Early this morning the Lord directed me to a verse of Scripture.'' He scooped up Luther's translation of the Bible. ''Listen to what Solomon, the wisest of men, had to say:

'''Train up a child in the way he should go: and when he is old, he will not depart from it' (Proverbs 22:6). For over a month I've been pulling that staghorn knife out of Andreas' middle.'' He closed the Bible and buttered a slice of bread. ''The poor boy swallowed it nearly a year and a half ago. His parents took him to other doctors. They called doctor after doctor.'' He rubbed his right ear. ''The blockheads tried to ease it out with olive oil and beer. Imagine trying to get a knife out of a boy's stomach with beer!

''After the doctors all failed, his father brought him to me. The knife had worked its way through his stomach and its handle was barely sticking out of a blister just beneath his heart. I immediately saw the solution. I tied a silk thread to the handle and have been slowly pulling it out. Last week I moved it half an inch.'' He turned toward his son.

''George Frideric has not swallowed a knife. But he's swallowed something much worse.'' He wagged his finger, and his lips became taut. ''George Frideric, the son of my old age, has swallowed the idea that he will study music.''

''Don't you like music, Papa?'' interrupted George Frideric.

Handel shrugged. ''Music is the least disagreeable of noises. But that's not the point. The point is: God made us all different. The Bachs are musicians. The Handels are doctors, lawyers, merchants.''

Anna placed the musical toys on the table before the seventy-year-old surgeon.

"Did you get all of them?" demanded the old man.

"I got all of the musical things that were in his room. I even crawled under his bed to get those sheets on which he was writing some music to play for your next birthday."

"Very well. All of you can now watch while I cast this musical demon into the fire." He removed the bellows from the top of the fireplace and blew the smoldering coals into a blaze. Then he grabbed the drum. His lips tight, he studied it for a moment, then dropped it back onto the table and picked up his Bible.

"Maybe we'd better learn what Jesus had to say about these matters," he said. "Ah, here's the passage." Raising his voice he read: "And if thy right hand offend thee, cut it off, and cast it from thee: for it is profitable for thee that one of thy members should perish, and not that thy whole body should be cast into hell" (Matthew 5:29). After snapping the Bible shut, he tossed the drum into the fire. Next, he threw in the whistle, the little stringed instrument, the small trumpet George Frideric had purchased with his own money and the music sheets smudged with a few lines of penciled notes.

As George Frideric watched his old friends crumple and turn into ash, it seemed that parts of his own body were being burned. Following several attempts to control himself, he sobbed, "Papa, I-I w-want to be g-good." He wiped his eyes.

"Then you will be a lawyer."

"But I want to learn music."

"George Frideric Handel," replied his father, "you will be a lawyer. That's my wish, and that's what you will do." He lifted his son's hand and spread his fingers. "I would rather that each of your fingers were cut off than for you to become a musician."

A look of horror twisted George Frideric's face.

"Why?" he asked as he suppressed a sob.

"Because musicians are beggars. They starve, hide in attics, beg. All they do is entertain brainless blockheads. Lawyers are rich. They wear fine clothes. They have carriages. But we'd better start eating." He mumbled a quick blessing and piled his plate with bacon and eggs.

George Frideric tried to eat, but it was impossible. His food was tasteless. Through tears he glanced around the table. His mother and her sister, Aunt Anna, were as expressionless as stumps. And his five-year-old sister Dorothea Sophia had a bewildered look on her face. As for two-year-old Johanna Christina, she was playing with a lid in her crib.

"You'd better eat," urged Handel, pointing at him with a fork.

George Frideric tried. It was wasted effort. Then he felt a warm touch on his elbow. Looking down, he saw his large grey cat. "What's the matter, Peter?" he asked, looking into his great yellow eyes.

Peter nudged him with his paw again. Then he whispered a short meow and began to purr.

"Would you like some bacon?"

The pathetic look in Peter's eyes indicated that he would.

"All right, my friend, here's a whole slice."

Peter had just finished the bacon and was scrubbing his face when there came a loud thump at the door. His father disappeared to investigate, and George Frideric noticed that Aunt Anna was trying to get his attention. When their eyes met, the trace of a smile edged her lips. Then she winked, nodded gently toward the attic, and her smile widened.

Puzzled, George Frideric frowned.

Again their eyes met. Again Anna winked and nodded toward the attic. Next, when his mother's eyes turned toward the door, Anna wriggled her fingers as if she were playing a clavichord.

All at once the lightning of understanding struck. George Frideric's response was immediate. He scooped his plate full of bacon and eggs and filled a saucer with milk for Peter. "It's time to eat," he said. When the main platter was empty, George Frideric said to Anna, "Please ask the cook to make some more bacon and eggs. I'm hungry. And ask him to bring some more milk for Peter."

George Frideric was in the act of refilling Peter's saucer when his father strode into the room. "Rudloff, Andreas' father, wants me to hurry over to his home. The boy is very sick. Dorothea, you'd better come with me. I may need someone to hold the poor boy. The rest of you will have to go to church by yourselves." He reached for his hat and then paused at the door. "Make sure that you sit in a back pew."

"Back pew! Why?" asked Anna, a frown soiling her thin, sharp face.

"Because when we sit near the front George Frideric concentrates on the organist. He seems to think that Herr Zachow is the most important person on earth."

Snuggled deeply in his winter coat, George Frideric held Anna's left hand while Dorothea Sophia gripped the other. The Lutheran *Our Lady's Church* was only a five minute walk from their large, three-storied, corner home in the Schlamm—one of Halle's finest suburbs.

Near the fountain in the cobbled square, a cloud of pigeons suddenly erupted. They fluttered briefly and settled nearby. After Dorothea Sophia broke loose to feed them the crumbs she had brought, Anna turned to George Frideric. In a low voice she said, "Your father told me to bring down the musical toys

that were in *your room*." She chuckled. "That's what
I did. He doesn't know about the clavichord in the
attic."

"That means I can still practice."

"Of course! Other than Peter, you and I are the
only ones who know it's there." She crossed her lips
with her finger. "But you must be careful that no one
hears you."

George Frideric smiled. "I knew when you winked
at me during breakfast." He was silent for two or three
steps. Then he said, "Aunt Anna, do you think Papa
will ever change his mind? I don't want to be a lawyer.
I want to be a musician."

"We worship a mighty God. He can change your
father's heart. We must pray. Martin Luther's father
also wanted him to be a lawyer. But God changed
things around so that he became a monk." Since
Dorothea had started toward them, Anna finished in
a whisper.

They approached the massive church which stood
in the left part of the square. Cornered by four high
towers, it resembled a backless chair that had been
turned upside down. George Frideric followed his aunt
through the heart-shaped door and sat with her on
the last pew in the rear. But even from that distance
he had a fine view of the organ whose massive pipes
reached like enormous fingers to the high, curved
ceiling.

Soon the sanctuary was filled with worshipers, many
of whom were George Frideric's special friends. He
smiled at Helmet and Hans, the Schmidt twins, and
nodded at freckled Herman Mann, whose father was
their butcher. He had played marbles with these
friends, gone with them on hikes, and fished with them
on the banks of the Saale. Soon the great organ
trembled into life and the congregation became silent.

George Frideric's fingers began to imitate those of the organist. The pew in front was his organ. As his fingers moved back and forth, he felt as if he were the organist. Swelling notes moved up and down, slowed, speeded, trilled, thundered, and at last sank into silence. George Frideric came to himself again and prayed, "Dear God, help Papa to change his mind."

The pastor's sermon was on overcoming difficulties. "The life of a Christian," he began, "is not easy. This is 1692. Two centuries ago Christopher Columbus fulfilled his boyhood dreams by crossing an unknown ocean. Did he have difficulties? He had many. He had to raise money from an antagonistic public to buy ships. He had to sail without charts. He had to put up with unbelieving seamen. Yet he continued on until he discovered the New World. What was his secret? He believed in God!"

The man in the black robe in the high pulpit continued with story after story about those who had been guided and used by the Lord. He referred to Paul, Augustine, Luther. Then he leaned dramatically forward and it seemed to George Frideric that his finger was jabbing at him.

"It may be that some of you young people— perhaps even children—in our congregation this morning feel called to do a special work for the Lord. Don't let anyone or any obstacle stop you. God delights in doing the impossible. The prophet Joel said, 'your old men shall dream dreams, your young men shall see visions' (2:28). Dreams and visions are sacred." The pastor drank a cup of water and continued.

"The Romans often entertained themselves by pushing Christians into the arena of the Colosseum and turning famished lions on them. Thousands were

killed. But sometimes as Christians awaited the lions,
they joined hands in front of the Emperor and sang
together as a choir:

> Glory be to the Father and to the Son,
>   and to the Holy Ghost;
> As it was in the beginning, is now
>   and ever shall be,
> World without end. Amen. Amen.

"Those martyrs whose blood reddened the floor of
the Colosseum proved to the world that God
strengthens courageous men and women and boys and
girls who obey their dreams and visions. We will now
stand, and as Friedrich Wilhelm Zachow accompanies
us on the organ, pledge our agreement to those
immortal second century words."

Mighty organ sounds filled the building again.
George Frideric stood and sang with all the enthusiasm
he possessed. At the conclusion, as he sang "Amen.
Amen," he was so carried away, he felt as if he were
ascending into heaven. His eyes became moist with
tears.

Anna lingered in the church until everyone was
gone. Then she said to the children. "Now, let's go
up front. I want to show you where you were baptized." Pointing to the marble baptismal font, she said
to George Frideric, "You were baptized here on
February 24, 1685. That was the day after you were
born. I held you in my arms and then handed you
over to my father, your grandfather Pastor George
Taust. I watched as he sprinkled you with water and
called your name. That was one of the happiest days
of his life. He lived only a few months after that.

"Just before Grandpa died, he said to me, 'Anna,
I want you to see to it that George Frideric does
something useful in this world.'"

"And why didn't you sit at the front?" interrupted a voice.

Astonished, for he thought the church was empty, George Frideric found himself peering into the face of the organist. "George Handel told us that we had to sit in the back," explained Anna.

"Why?"

"Because he knows George Frideric is fascinated with you. And he is afraid his son will become a musician."

Zachow laughed and rubbed his hands. "Well, you're up here now. Let me show you the organ."

"Why are the pipes so big?" asked George Frideric.

"For different tones," replied Zachow as he scooted onto the organ bench. "The lower the tone, the taller and bigger the pipe; and the higher the tone, the shorter and smaller the pipe. Here, let me show you." He pressed the lowest note and then the highest.

"How tall is the lowest pipe?"

"Sixty feet."

"S-sixty f-f-f-feet! That sounds big."

"Right. Come up here and sit beside me and touch some of the keys."

Since the bench was too high, Anna lifted him into place.

George Frideric couldn't believe that he was actually sitting on the bench of a real organ. Gingerly, he touched the lowest key. The responding vibrations sent a stream a chills up his spine. Then he touched the highest note. The shrill sound that followed was so high he could just hear it. All at once a daring idea leaped into his head. Boldly, he touched middle C. Then with one finger at a time he played the melody of the morning's closing chorus:

Glory be to the Father, and to the Son . . .

Zachow stared. "Can you read music?" he asked.
"A little."

After a long silence, Zachow said, "Move over to the edge of the bench." Then in full harmony he played the first line of *A Mighty Fortress*. "Now, could you play that?"

Without answering, George Frideric, played as though on his clavichord at home. He played the melody, and harmony too.

A mighty fortress is our God . . .

He played without effort. His timing was perfect.

Zachow stared again. Then he licked his lips and thoughtfully patted his freshly-powdered wig. Finally, after moistening his lips again, he asked, "George Frideric, have you taken lessons?"

"N-no."

Zachow stared some more. Then he said, "Miss Taust, your nephew is extremely talented. He *must* take music lessons."

"I agree," replied Anna. "But his father is against it. And, as you know, George Handel can be stubborn."

Zachow smiled knowingly. "I understand. But God can change him. Let's agree in prayer that He will do just that."

2
Patience

As George Frideric viewed the Sunday table loaded with roast, fish, creamed puddings, steaming vegetables, pies, and an assortment of breads, he was so hungry he could hardly wait for his father to say the blessing. Then he glanced at Dorothea Sophia and his mouth went dry.

Why, oh why hadn't he warned her not to say anything about how he had played the church organ? From the time she learned to talk, his sister was generally the first to relay anything new. And now her brown eyes were brimming with mischief.

George Handel had just finished saying grace when Dorothea Sophia said, "Papa, you should have been in church with us this morning."

"Yes, you should have been there," interrupted George Frideric. "The pastor preached a good sermon. But I've been wondering, Papa, how did you do with the knife? Did you get it all out?"

"Not quite. The handle is out. Now I have to remove the blade. I'm going to see him again tomor-

row. Why don't you come along? You might be able
to help.''

"How could I help?''

"You could hold Andreas' hand while I pull.''

"What time are you leaving?''

"Nine.''

"Will the horses be ready?''

"Of course.''

"Has the carriage been fixed? Yesterday, a wheel
almost came off.''

"It's ready.''

"My leather pants have a hole in them.''

"Wear another pair.''

"When will we—''

"Why all the questions?'' asked his father a little
gruffly. He refilled his plate with fish.

"I-I-I want to help as m-much as possible.'' George
Frideric glanced at his sister. Her eyes were popping.
He could almost see the dreaded story bubbling within
her. He lowered his head while he tried to think of
a way to get her mind on another subject.

Soon the family was eating again. George Frideric
had just finished swallowing three bites of roast when
his sister began. "Papa, you should have been with
us in church. Anna took us to the front where Grandpa
baptized George Frideric. While we were there, Herr
Zachow came over and—''

"How long is the knife in Andreas?'' asked George
Frideric.

"About two inches, I think. But don't interrupt
your sister. Go on, Dorothea Sophia. What did the
organist do?''

George Frideric closed his eyes and held his breath.

"He showed us the organ—''

"And he told us that one of the pipes is sixty feet
tall,'' interrupted George Frideric. "He's certainly

a nice man. Papa, we should invite him and his wife over for d-d-dinner.''

Handel frowned. ''George Frideric, keep still. I want to hear the story from your sister.''

''Yes, Papa.''

''After he told us about the organ,'' continued his sister, ''Aunt Anna helped George Frideric get up on the bench. And do you know what he did?''

''What?''

''He played some songs. And Herr Zachow said he should take music lessons.''

''Is that so?'' demanded Handel, turning to Anna.

''Yes, that's the way it was. Zachow even said that your son is talented.'' She bit her lip and looked down.

''Mmmmm. Well, I've made up my mind, and my son is going to be a lawyer.'' He got up from the table and unhooked his leather strap from the nail by the fireplace. He swung it back and forth several times. Then he returned it to the nail. ''No, that won't help,'' he muttered half to himself. He paced back and forth in deep thought. Finally, he said, ''George Frideric, I will show you something tomorrow that will flush this idea of music out of your head.''

George Frideric tried to eat. But he only managed to clean up a fourth of his plate. Then he felt a warm paw on his elbow. ''All right, Peter,'' he said, ''it's all yours.'' He scraped the leftovers into Peter's thick plate by the kitchen door. Then he excused himself from the table. ''I'm going to my room,'' he explained.

While George Frideric was stretched out on his bed in deep thought, the door slowly inched open. Peter crept in and jumped up on the bed.

''Peter, you're the best friend I have,'' said George Frideric as he stroked him.

Peter responded by rubbing whiskers against his face.

"Now I'm in trouble and you must help me. Papa is angry because I played the organ at church. He doesn't want me to be a musician. Please tell me how I can change his mind."

Peter winked one eye and purred even louder.

"You know you must help me. Last year when I found you shivering on Barefoot Monk's Street I brought you home and fed you. If it weren't for me you'd be a dead cat."

Peter crawled up on George Frederic's chest, meowed, rubbed his whiskers on each of George Frederic's cheeks and licked his chin.

"When I first brought you home, Papa didn't like you. He said you'd bring in fleas and he threatened to throw you in the river. But Papa's not angry at you anymore. How did you do it?"

Peter closed both eyes, curled up on his stomach, and continued to purr.

"Tell me, Peter, how did you change his mind?"

Instead of replying with even a faint meow, Peter simply relaxed and sank into a deep sleep.

"You're not a very thankful cat." he scolded. "I save your life, feed you, pet you, talk to you, and all you do is sleep."

Peter's only response was to sleepily wink first his left eye and then his right eye. George Frideric shook his head. Then suddenly he exclaimed, "Oh, I see, you *are* telling me something. How stupid I've been not to understand until now."

"You don't lay eggs, yet you're fed. You don't give milk, yet you're fed. You don't pull a carriage, yet you're fed. You wouldn't be good to eat, yet you're fed. How do you manage to live so well without giving anything in return? I know. You do it with patience and love. All right, Peter, my friend, you've taught me a lesson. I'm going to have patience and love."

A little later he lifted Peter from his stomach and put him on the end of the bed. "I'm going to the attic," he whispered to the sleeping cat.

George Frideric tiptoed past his parents' bedroom and quietly climbed the narrow back steps to the attic. There, in a bright stream of light, was his clavichord. The piano-like upright had been used by nuns in a convent. Anna had helped him find the little instrument and secretly take it up the steps to the attic. They had muffled the notes so that almost no one other than the player could hear it.

Sitting on a low stool, George Frideric played *A Mighty Fortress* with one finger. Then he practiced adding harmony with his left hand. He had been practicing for about an hour when the door squeaked open.

His heart fluttering, George Frideric stared. Then he relaxed. It was Peter! The cat rubbed up against him, stretched, and yawned. "Don't swallow me," said George Frideric.

Peter had heard that remark before and ignored it. Totally unconcerned, he sat near his master's feet, licked the side of his paw, scrubbed his whiskers, activated his purring machine, and went to sleep. After more practice, George Frideric cradled Peter in his arms, closed the door, tiptoed downstairs and poured him some milk.

On Monday, George Frideric washed and checked in the mirror. The face he saw in the glass had brown eyes, firm eyebrows, a solid chin and a thin nose with a slight rise at the end. Quickly, he ran a comb through his dark hair and went to the table. Before seating himself, he checked his silver shoe-buckles and the buttons that gripped his knickers just below his knees.

"We're going to leave early," warned his father. "On the way I'll show you some things of family interest."

Dressed in the black garb of a surgeon, Handel reined the horses at *Unter den Kleinschmieden* (Street of the Small Smith). Pointing with the handle of his whip, he said, "Your grandfather learned to be a coppersmith and operated a little shop here."

"Grandfather?"

"Yes. My father, Valentine Handel. He was a hard worker. He owned several houses. He had five sons. Two died. The other two, your uncles, became coppersmiths like him. But I became a doctor."

"Why didn't you become a coppersmith, too?"

"Shaping copper didn't interest me." As George Handel spoke about the past, his enthusiasm increased. "In my later teens I began to see that the best thing I could do was to help others. Then, after I had been shaving for a few years, I became an apprentice to Christoph Oettinger. He was a barber-surgeon. I lived in his home. He taught me how to cut hair and do surgery. He also taught me the importance of money. He used to say, 'The main purpose of money is to make more money. Get as much as you can, and keep it. Money is power.'

"I learned that lesson from him. That's the reason we have such a comfortable home. When Herr Oettinger died, I married his widow." He chuckled. "Anna was a fine woman. She gave me six children. We were married forty years. Then Anna died of the plague. She was a true Christian. The next year I married your mother Dorothea Taust. I was almost sixty-one at the time.

"Friends asked why I remarried when I was so old. I told them I wanted to have a son who would do important work, such as law. Ah, but now we've arrived at Herr Rudloff's place."

The Rudloff home was out in the country. A flock of ducks quacked as Handel tethered the horses to a post. "And how's Andreas?" inquired the surgeon.

"You're saving his life, my friend," replied the boy's father.

As he looked at the boy's middle with the handle of the knife protruding, George Frideric asked, "And how did you swallow it?"

"I was running with the knife in my mouth when I tripped over a brick," replied the sixteen-year-old boy.

Gingerly Handel examined the stag-horn and the bit of blade that had emerged. Then he said, "While George Frideric holds your hand, I'm going to pull the rest of it out. There may be a lot of pain. But, you'll be rid of the knife."

Slowly the seventy-year-old surgeon pulled, rested, pulled some more, and rested again. After a little over two hours of careful work the knife was out.

Herr Rudloff studied the dagger from several angles and shook his head in disbelief. "It's a miracle!" he exclaimed. "That thing was in him for one year, thirty weeks, and three days. Herr Handel, you are the greatest surgeon in Germany."

As they were heading back to Halle, George Handel was in a mountain-top mood. "The greatest satisfactions in life come from helping others," he said. "Your half brother Gottfried was a great surgeon. He could cut hair better than anyone else and he knew just how to bleed his patients. Oh, I wish he were alive today. But the plague got him. Do you know why he was so great?"

"Why?"

"Because I told him what to do, and he listened. You will listen too. You will be a lawyer. You will be rich and help people. Think how good you would feel if you saved a man from the gallows."

George Frideric remembered Peter's lesson of

patience. He remained silent during the rest of the trip back to Halle.

After practicing all afternoon on his hidden clavichord, George Frideric went to his room. As his mind puzzled over how he would change Papa's mind, Peter crawled onto his chest and began to purr.

"This time you must help me," said George Frederic, a note of authority in his voice. "You know how to get people to feed you. Now show me how to get Papa to let me take music lessons. Please!"

Peter replied with a low meow and increased the volume of his purrs.

"As I told you before, you know how to win friends.

You rub against people's legs, purr, touch elbows with your paw, and look sad. Tell me, your majesty, Herr Peter, what should I do?''

Peter's only reply was to sleep with just the tip of his tongue showing. But as he slept, he kept rumbling like a waterfall.

While George Frideric continued to stroke his friend, he suddenly had an idea. Leaping out of bed, he took his startled companion downstairs, poured him some milk, and headed to the home of the organist.

Zachow was weeding his garden.

"Papa refuses for me to take music lessons," he blurted.

"That's a shame. You're quite talented."

"Please, Herr Zachow, next Sunday after service I'm going to persuade Papa to go with me to the baptismal font. Could you invite us to the organ and let me play *A Mighty Fortress*."

Zachow frowned. "Sounds like a, a con-conspiracy." He laughed.

"Please!"

"All right, I will. I always like to please fellow musicians."

That afternoon George Frideric got out his father's Sunday shoes and polished them until they glistened.

"Why are you doing that?" asked Anna suspiciously.

"Because I want Papa to be happy."

3
Dead-End Street

Sitting next to his father, George Frideric leaned forward as the pastor preached on the Scripture lesson: "For my thoughts are not your thoughts, neither are your ways my ways, saith the Lord" (Isaiah 55:8).

"These words of the prophet explain that God often works in ways we do not understand," preached the man in the pulpit. "For example, when He needed a brave man to prove to the world that we are saved by faith and not good works, He selected Martin Luther. Ah, but on that occasion God had a problem.

"God's problem was that Hans Luther insisted that his son become a lawyer. Nonetheless, He solved that problem." The pastor paused in order to quench his thirst. George Frideric studied his father's face out of the corner of his eye. It was tense. "Yes, God has a way of solving problems," repeated the man in the dark robe. "While young Martin Luther was away on a trip, he was slammed to the earth by a stroke of lightning. After he regained his feet, he exclaimed: 'Saint Anne, help me. I will become a monk.'

"It was in this fashion that God prepared the way for the Reformation."

The pastor continued. For half an hour he related instances in which God removed obstacles that hindered His plan. Then, as he drew near to the close of his sermon, he said, "After the Reformation began sweeping Europe, God needed special music to motivate His children, to put a spring in their step. Great music, as we all know, is often born in the darkest pits of despair.

"Doctor Luther at this time was enduring the most painful period of his life. He was under sentence of death. And while he feared being burned alive at the stake, the peasants turned against him. They called him *Doctor Lügner*—(Doctor Liar). He suffered indescribable pain from kidney stones, earaches, dizziness. The plague all but closed the university where he taught. It dropped down to one hundred students. Many of his friends died of the disease. And he had financial troubles.

"His boarders did not pay their bills, and Luther could not meet his obligations. Moreover, no one would lend him any money. In addition, Suleiman the Magnificent had invaded Europe and was cutting through it as a hot knife cuts through butter. Sulieman was determined to replace our churches with mosques.

"But that wasn't all. Elizabeth, his eight-month-old daughter, died in his arms. Indeed, Doctor Luther was so downcast he cried out: 'Satan rages against me with his whole might, and the Lord has put me in his power like another Job. The devil tempts me with great infirmity of spirit. Every night devils come into this place. They make noises, rattle chains. I can hear them.'

"One day, while deep in the slime of despair, this former monk signed his name to a letter with the words, *Christi lutum* (Christ's mud).

"Then in this blackest of black moments while his teeth were throbbing with the pains of hell, God gave Doctor Luther the great hymn, *Ein' Feste Burg* (A Mighty Fortress). He slowly swept his eyes over the congregation. "And now we will sing that hymn, the battle-cry of the Reformation. We will all stand while Herr Zachow makes the organ leap with power."

As he clasped his father's hand, and his imagination knocked at the gates of heaven, George Frideric sang with all the volume he could manage:

> A mighty fortress is our God,
> a bulwark never failing;
> Our helper He amid the flood
> of mortal ills prevailing.

At the end of the fourth verse, George Frideric felt as if he were gripped in an ever-tightening vise. His mind seemed locked in Luther's study at Wittenberg. He even had visions of him dipping his quill in the ink and writing, *'Ein' Feste Burg ist unser Gott.'* Then he remembered his plans, "Papa," he said as he tugged at his father's hand, "let's go up front and see where Grandpa Taust baptized me."

"It's getting late. We don't have time." George Handel started for the door.

"Just this once. Please!" George Frideric imitated Peter as he looked into his father's eyes.

"Oh, all right."

While they lingered at the baptismal font, Zachow approached. "Glad to see you, Herr Handel," he greeted, grasping his hand. "I hear you got the knife out of Andreas."

"I did."

"The whole city of Halle is praising you. You worked a miracle."

"Thanks."

"Herr Handel, I want you to have a closer look at the organ. It's one of the finest in Germany. Your father helped pay for it. He was a most generous man." Zachow adjusted his wig. "How did you like Luther's great hymn?"

Handel shrugged. "It was all right."

While they were speaking, Zachow swung George Frideric onto the organ bench. "Let's see if you can play that hymn," he said. He pointed to the triple-keyboard.

George Frideric gulped. This was the moment for which he had planned. Now was his chance. He must not make a mistake. Not one. As he reached out his hands, he could feel his father's eyes burning into the back of his head. Nonetheless, he must do his best. Playing the melody with his right hand, he added chords with his left hand. He went through one verse completely without error. While in the middle of the second verse his father shouted, "Stop!"

"Is something wrong?" asked Zachow.

"I'm the victim of a plot!" stormed Handel.

"Herr Handel, your son has great talent," said Zachow. He spoke softly and smiled. "He should take music lessons."

"My son will be a lawyer, Herr Zachow. He will not take music lessons."

"Ah, but Herr Handel, George Frideric's talent should not be wasted."

"His talent *will* be wasted if he becomes a musician. He's the son of my old age. I want him to be able to lift his head in the world."

"Over at Eisenach, Johann Ambrosius Bach has a son who was born just a month after George Frideric. I saw Ambrosius last week and you should have heard him brag about Johann Sebastian. He says that he's a musical genius."

"That's fine," replied Handel. There was an edge of sarcasm in his voice. "But please remember, Herr Zachow, they are Bachs. They've been musicians for generations. I'm a Handel. My father was a Handel. My grandfather was a Handel. My son is a Handel. Now please, don't encourage him to become a musician." With Dorothea Sophia hanging to his left hand, and with his right hand firmly gripping that of George Frideric, he headed for home. As he stomped by the fountain, the pigeons may have sensed his anger, for they all flew away and settled on the front towers of the church.

Since dinner was not yet on the table, George Frideric hurried to his room. Stretched out on the bed, he began to sob. As his mind reviewed his troubles, Peter settled by his side.

"It's isn't fair, Peter," sobbed George Frideric. Peter didn't answer.

"It's this way," continued George Frideric, while stroking the cat's head and back. "God made you a cat. Now how would you like it if I made you bark like a dog or moo like a cow? Of course you wouldn't like it. But that's what's happening to me. When I'm grown up I want to play a great organ, one that has pipes at least sixty feet tall."

If Peter understood this, he didn't let on.

"So you're not going to answer me." George Frideric continued to stroke him and rub his ears and whiskers. "Well, that's all right." While he was petting him, Peter turned over and George Frideric's hand went across his stomach.

"My, you have a big stomach!" he exclaimed. "You must be eating too much. You'd better go on a diet or your stomach will be dragging the floor."

The dinner bell bonged, and George Frideric hurriedly washed his face and dabbed his eyes with cold water so no one would know that he'd been crying.

The table was loaded with good things. "Have some beef," suggested Aunt Anna. George Frideric took a tiny portion. "That's not enough to keep a chicken alive," said his mother. "Here, let me get you some fish."

"No, thanks. I don't want any fish. I'm not hungry."

Peter touched his elbow. "No, Peter," he said. "You're getting too fat." Peter touched him again, meowed, purred, and assumed such a pathetic look, he broke down. "Oh, all right. You can have everything on my plate."

At the end of the meal, George Handel said, "Son, I've arranged for you to start attending the Lutheran Gymnasium. I've instructed the teacher in charge that he's not to teach you any music nor to allow you to play any musical instrument. Is that clear?"

"Yes, Papa."

"Also, I told him to give you extra assignments, especially in Latin."

"Why?"

"Because all lawyers need to know Latin."

That night, as George Frideric knelt by his bed for his evening prayers, he prayed for everyone except his father. He even remembered Herr Zachow and Peter. Feeling smug about not having prayed for his father, he slipped into bed. But he could not sleep. He twisted from side to side. tried to sleep on his stomach; placed his head at the foot, and even tried to sleep crosswise. Nothing worked. Finally, he got out of bed, knelt on the floor, and repeated his evening prayer. This time, he prayed for his father.

Ten minutes later, he was sound asleep.

4
Strange Twists

George Frideric liked school. But he couldn't keep his mind away from music. His ears were always alert for the chiming of church bells, the songs of birds, the ripple of water, the chirp of crickets, and even the sighing of trees.

Every subject reminded him of music.

"Why is Hamburg a famous city?" asked the teacher.

"Because of its great music and opera," replied George Frideric.

"Who was John Hus?"

"He was the Bohemian martyr who sang while he was being burned alive. He was put to death because he taught that the wine in the Lord's Supper is for everyone."

"Why is it important to learn mathematics?"

"So as to keep time while playing a musical instrument."

"Why do all Protestants remember Wittenberg?"

"Because that's where Doctor Luther composed *Ein' Feste Burg*."

The teachers attempted to get George Frideric to stop answering their questions in such fashion. But although he tried to comply, it was wasted effort. After a long lecture on how Doctor Luther had translated the New Testament into German while hiding in the Wartburg Fortress at Eisenach, the teacher had a question. "Why is Eisenach an important city for Lutherans?" he asked.

"Because that's the home of the Bachs," replied George Frideric before he could stop himself.

The teacher scowled. But before he managed another question, George Frideric's hand went up.

"Yes, George Frideric."

"How long would it take a man's breath to reach from Eisenach to Halle?"

"That would depend on the direction of the wind and the speed it was blowing."

"What if it were blowing in a northeasterly direction at say ten miles an hour. How long would that take?"

"Maybe eight hours. But why would you want to know that?"

George Frideric did not reply. Instead, he slumped down in his seat and a curious smile crossed his face.

One morning at breakfast, George Frideric stared at Peter. "What's happened to you?" he asked. "You were getting so fat your middle was dragging the floor, and now you're so narrow I can see your ribs. Are you sick?" Instead of answering, Peter touched him with his paw. George Frideric gave him a slice of bacon, but Peter wanted more and then more and even more.

That Saturday after school, George Frideric climbed a tall tree in the school yard. He seated himself comfortably in the tree and searched the distant, southwesterly horizon. Perhaps he could see the top

of the church steeple at Eisenach. It was wasted effort.
*Well, if he couldn't see with his eyes, he would see with his
imagination.*

Daydreaming, he imagined that he was Johann
Sebastian Bach, and that he was taking lessons on the
great Eisenach church organ. As his dreams expanded,
he took deep breaths, hoping that perhaps the Bachs
had breathed the same air earlier in the day.

While enjoying his fantasies, George Frideric was
suddenly aware of a stream of ants climbing up his
legs. Soon they were chewing his tender skin. Gritting his teeth, he began to slap at them. ''Take that
and that and that you miserable wretches!'' He
shouted. But it was a lost battle. He squirmed out of
his perch and headed for the ground. On the way
down, his newly mended leather britches were torn
on the stump of a branch.

Since the hole in his britches was not large, George
Frideric headed for his customary seat in the outside
vestibule of the church. Sitting there, just outside the
heart-shaped front door, he was able to hear snatches
of the organ as Herr Zachow practiced for the Sunday services. As he listened, Helmet and Hans
Schmidt approached.

''We're going fishing,'' announced Hans. ''Why
don't you come along?''

''It's too hot.''

''It's cool by the river.''

''Maybe so. But I like it here.''

That evening as Aunt Anna mended his torn
britches, she asked, ''How did you tear them?''

''I was up in a tree daydreaming,'' replied George
Frideric.

Anna started to say something, reconsidered, and
continued with her sewing. After the new leather patch
was secured, she said, ''Your father is very deter-

mined." she sucked in her breath and shook her head.
"I remember when he used to come to our house to
see your mother. Since he was past sixty, and thirty
years older than your mother, a lot of people shook
their heads. But age and talk mean nothing to George.
His first wife was ten years older than he. Your father
never gives up."

"How will I change his mind?"

"I-I d-don't know." She handed him the mended
britches. "Best way would be to get some important
person he respects to persuade him."

"How about you and Mother?"

"Never! He's the head of the house. Neither of us
count. Nor would the pastor or even Herr Zachow."
She thoughtfully tapped her teeth. "The one who
might change him is the Duke of Weissenfels. I said
might. The Duke likes music, your father likes the
Duke, and your half brother George Christian Handel
is the Duke's valet de chambre. That means he looks
after his clothes and is thus very close to him. Your
father often goes to visit your half brother."

"But, Aunt Anna, how would I get the Duke to
change him?"

The only way would be for the Duke to hear you
play."

"And how would he get to hear me play?"

"Maybe when your father goes to Weissenfels for
a visit you could go along."

"When will he go?"

"I've no idea. But while you're waiting for your
chance, keep practicing on your clavichord, and keep
praying."

After a hard week of examinations, George Frideric
was practicing in the attic when the door opened. His
heart in his throat, he stared through the
semidarkness. Then he relaxed. It was Peter and he
had a bundle in his mouth.

"You shouldn't bring a rat up here!" exclaimed George Frideric.

Peter ignored the statement and crept into the nearby closet. A moment later, without his load, and with something obviously on his mind, he slipped out the door and disappeared. Soon he was back with another load, and then another, and another. After the fourth trip he remained in the closet.

Curious, George Frideric opened the closet door. What he saw widened his eyes. Peter was curled up on a rug and was vigorously washing a set of kittens. In and out, in and out went his tongue as he scrubbed their little faces. And, as he worked, he entertained the kittens with loud purrs.

George Frideric shook his head. "Where did you get those kittens?" he demanded. Instead of answering, Peter turned on his side and the four kittens found their places at the lunch counter he displayed before them. "And so you're not a tomcat as I had thought," marvelled George Frideric. "Since that's the case, Peter is not a good name for you. From now on you are Petrina."

Two of the kittens were white with slightly greyish front paws and two of them were a solid grey just like their mother. Petrina kept her family in the attic closet for two or three weeks and then she lifted each by the nape of the neck and moved them to another closet in the basement.

George Frideric continued the routine of going to school, daydreaming in the vestibile of the church, and practicing on the hidden clavichord. One evening Petrina showed up at the table with her four kittens marching in single file just behind her.

"Why is she so thin?" asked George Frideric.

"Because she's nursing kittens," explained his father.

Soon, Petrina was at George Frideric's side begging. "Here's some meat and a bit of fish," he said,
handing her generous pieces. But instead of eating
the handouts, Petrina gave them to her kittens.

George Frideric frowned. "Why does she do that?"
he asked.

"Because she's weaning them," replied his mother.

"You see, it's more blessed to give than to receive,"
commented Aunt Anna.

Everyone laughed.

Petrina's kittens grew up and were given away.
Then she had another litter and then another. Each
time the routine was the same.

One spring afternoon, George Frideric was practicing on the clavichord when the door swung wide.
Looking up, he stared into the face of his father.

"I thought I told you that you were not to play any
musical instruments!" he all but yelled.

George Frideric's breath stopped and a vacuum
formed in his stomach. Never before had he seen such
lines of anger on his father's face. "Yes, Father," he
gulped. Then he began to sob.

Arms akimbo, his father glared. "Come, let's go
downstairs." He grabbed him by the arm and led him
down the steps. At the foot, he said, "From this time
on you are to stay out of the attic. Do you
understand?"

"Yes, Papa."

"What did I say?"

"I'm to stay out of the attic."

Handel picked up the strap and thumped it on the
table. "And if you don't stay out of the attic, I'll tan
your hide. Is that clear?"

Unable to answer because of his tears, George
Frideric nodded. After his father had gone, he retired
to his room. As he was wiping his face, Petrina jumped

up on his bed and rubbed his cheek with her whiskers.
"Petrina," he said, as he stroked her, "I'm puzzled
about my father."

"Meow?" she asked.

"Yes, I'm puzzled about him. Why didn't he give
me a beating?" He was thoughtfully silent for a long
moment. Then, half to himself he asked, "Do you
suppose he thinks that by opposing me he will make
me even more determined to be a musician?"

In answer, Petrina settled on his chest, winked one
eye, increased the volume of her purrs, and went to
sleep with the tip of her tongue hanging out.

For several weeks after this, George Frideric retired
to his room early each afternoon; and, daydreaming,
imagined that his bed was an organ. As his fingers
went back and forth across the bed, Petrina studied
him with big yellow eyes. She never said a word. But
she seemed interested with her short meows, rubs,
licks, and deep-throated purrs.

Early one summer morning during school vacation,
George Frideric missed his father at the breakfast
table. "Where's Papa?" he asked.

"He's on his way to Weissenfels," replied Anna.

"To see the Duke?"

"He's gone to see your half brother. But I'm sure
he'll also see the Duke."

"Would you like to go with him?" interrupted his
mother somewhat eagerly.

"More than anything."

"Well, why don't you go out and see if you can
catch up with him?" His mother's voice had a curious
tone. It sounded as if she wanted him to try and catch
up with his father.

"But he's in a carriage. I can't run as fast as
horses."

"The roads are rather muddy from the rain last

night. You just might catch up with him," said Anna.

"When did he leave?"

"About half an hour ago."

"Then I'm going to catch up with him." George crammed his mouth full of bacon and eggs. "Give the rest to Petrina," he said over his shoulder. He jerked the door open, but his mother stopped him. "You'll need a change of clothing," she said. "Take this." She handed him a small suitcase. "I packed your Sunday best in that."

Weissenfels was about twenty-five miles to the south on the other side of the Saale. George Frideric had never been there, but since there was only one road, he knew he could find the way. He sped over the road and kept watching the horizon for a sign of the carriage. Soon he was out of breath.

Perhaps someone would come by on a horse and pick him up. No one did. On, on he ran. Then he saw the carriage. It was stopped at the top of a hill.

"W-what h-happened?" panted George Frideric.

"A wheel came off," replied his father. "But it's all right. The coachman will fix it." He glanced at the suitcase. "Did I forget something?"

"N-no."

"I brought along a change of clothes. I was h-hoping I-I could s-see my brother."

"How did you know that I was going to Weissenfels?"

"I didn't."

"Who packed your suitcase?"

"I-I d-don't k-know."

"Mmmmm. I think I smell another rat." He brushed his black suit with his hand. "I've a good notion to take you back home." He glanced at the coachman as he worked on the wheel. "No. George Christian is expecting me."

"You mean I'll get to see the Duke?" George Frideric's voice rumbled with excitement.

"Of course." A deep frown smudged Handel's face. "But I thought your main interest was in seeing your brother."

George Frideric bit his lip. "I-I w-w-w-want to see b-both of them."

"Mmmmm. " Handel pinched his nose. "Yes, I smell a clever rat!"

As George Frideric tiptoed around the living room of the Duke's palace, he was amazed at the enormous chandeliers, colored windows, luxurious carpets, oil paintings, and glistening furniture. For a while he stood in awe before a magnificent painting. Then his eyes settled on the largest clavichord he had ever seen.

"The organist at Halle tells me that you are an extremely talented musician," said the Duke. "Why don't you play something?"

George Frideric swallowed hard and glanced at his father. His father's face had hardened into grim lines. Not knowing what to do, he hesitated. But the Duke made it easy for him. "Don't be modest," he said. "Play. That's an order."

Silently, George Frideric prayed. Then boldly he seated himself on the bench and with both hands played *Ein' Feste Berg*. This clavichord was much better than the one in the attic, and the music filled the room.

"That was great!" exclaimed the Duke. "Now play it again."

After George Frideric had complied, the Duke clapped for a servant. "Summon the church organist," he said. "Tell him to come here immediately."

While George Frideric awaited the organist, he prayed that God would continue to help him. Finally the organist appeared. He was wearing a freshly-powdered wig. "You must hear this young genius play," said the Duke.

After bowing low, the organist seated himself on the sofa. "I'm ready," he announced.

The organist listened carefully as George Frideric played four or five selections. Then he asked, "How many lessons have you taken?"

"None."

"You have talent. You should take lessons immediately. If you lived here I'd be glad to teach you myself."

"Could he play something for the congregation at the end of the service?" asked the Duke.

"Certainly."

That night George Frideric had a hard time getting to sleep; and when he did he dreamed that while crawling through the organ's sixty-foot pipe he got stuck and was attacked by an army of ants.

After breakfast, George Frideric donned his best clothes, and noticed a bit of paper attached to them. The paper said: "Anna and I will be praying for you." It was signed: "Mother." He read the note three times, then folded it and put it in his pocket.

Yes, God was answering their prayers!

The church that morning was crowded and George Frideric tensely awaited the moment he would mount the organ bench. Then, almost before he knew it, the pastor said, "This morning we have a special treat. Herr George Frideric Handel, the eight-year-old son of George Handel the famous surgeon from Halle, will play for us on the organ."

As George Frideric faced the keys of the organ which he had never seen before, he was gripped by a terrible fright. *What would he do if he accidentally pressed the wrong keys? What would his father say if he failed; and, even worse, what would his father do if he succeeded?*

A glance in the organ's mirror revealed row after
row of eager listeners. Then he spotted his father. He
was sitting halfway back on the right side of the center
aisle. His face was clouded by a strange mixture of
dismay, pride, and resentment.

All at once George Frideric's heart calmed and he
had a vision of the Christians in the Roman Colosseum. As the ragged group stood before the emperor
awaiting the moment when the famished lions would
be turned on them, they suddenly began to sing a
hymn about immortality. Then his hands were on the
keyboard and he was playing the music that accompanies the famous lines:

> Glory be to the Father, and to the Son,
>   and to the Holy Ghost;
> As it was in the beginning, is now
>   and ever shall be,
> World without end. Amen. Amen.

When George Frideric concluded there was a
stunned silence. It was as if the world had come to
an end. Then the pastor signaled the congregation to
rise. "We've witnessed the beginning of a great
career," he said with a slight huskiness in his voice.

That afternoon the Duke approached George
Handel. Fixing him with his eyes, he asked, "Are you
giving your son music lessons?"

"No. My son will be a lawyer. I don't want him
to starve."

"Herr Handel," said the Duke, placing both hands
on the surgeon's shoulders, "your son will start taking lessons at once. This is an order."

George Handel gulped and his eyes widened as if
he were being choked. Finally, he said, "If that's an
order, my son will start taking music lessons. I am
your servant."

5

Harmony

On the way back to Halle, George Handel slipped his right arm around George Frideric. "God has spoken," he said. "You are destined to be a musician just as Martin Luther was destined to be a reformer. I shall arrange for you to study under Herr Zachow."

Zachow outlined a heavy schedule. "You're getting older each day," he explained. "The best time to learn is when you're young. And since you have the talent to become a great musician, I will be thorough." He gritted his teeth and patted his chin. "We will study the history of music, and we'll learn how music developed in the church. At the same time, we'll study harmony and counterpoint."

"And where will I take my lessons?" asked George Frideric.

"In the church. We'll use the church organ." His eyes slipped from George Frideric's head to his feet. "Your legs aren't long enough to reach the foot pedals. But boys have a way of growing. The secret of becom-

ing an effective musician is practice. Have you heard
of Scarlatti?''

''No. Who is he?''

''Alessandro Scarlatti is the greatest musician and
composer in Italy. From the beginning of his life he
was in love with music. He always listened to the birds
and musicians. He began lessons as soon as possible.
And he practiced day and night. Ah, but he had his
reward. He composed his first opera and directed it
himself in Rome when he was only twenty.'' Zachow
shook his head. ''If that were not so, I would not
believe it.''

''Right now I'm nine,'' said George Frideric.
''That means that if I'm to do as well as Scarlatti I'll
have to write and put on an opera within the next
eleven years. Do you think I can do that?''

Zachow laughed. ''Eleven years isn't very long.
You'll barely have whiskers by that time. But if a
person really wants to do something he can do it. That
is, if it is in the will of God.''

''Anything?''

''Anything!''

During his first lesson, George Frideric sat with
some other boys in front of the church near the organ.
He was by far the youngest in the group. ''To begin
our study,'' lectured Herr Zachow, ''all of us should
know that music is extremely important. A thousand
years ago, the Venerable Bede (673-735) wrote:
'Music is the most worthy, courteous, pleasant, joyous
and lovely of all knowledge. . . .Music encourages
us to bear the heaviest afflictions, administers con-
solation in every difficulty, refreshes the broken spirit,
removes headaches and cures crossness and
melancholy.'

''Music has a long history. Very ancient men, even
before Noah, invented musical instruments. In time,

men developed a system of musical *notation* so they could write on paper how the melody of a song should go. Notation changed across the centuries. But the invention of printing finally stopped the constant altering of the system. Thus, in our time a staff has five lines instead of from four to thirteen as it has had at other times.

"Music has always been important in the church. Luther, however, was one of the first reformers to put Christian words to popular tunes. John Calvin thoroughly disliked the idea of writing fresh words for hymns. He taught that we should only sing the psalms of David." Zachow shrugged. "Many Christians in the early centuries did not like to use musical instruments in church. The Venerable Bede insisted that music made by instruments was *artificial* while that made by voices alone was *natural*.

"Organs didn't come into the church until the tenth century. One of the first organs to be used was in Winchester, England. That organ had four hundred pipes and twenty-six bellows; and two organists were needed to play it. These men worked together and pounded the keys with their fists. That organ, I've been told, was so loud it could be heard all over the town." He laughed.

After the first lesson, George Frideric approached Herr Zachow. "Do you have a book that gives the history of music?" he inquired.

"I do. Stop at my house and I'll lend it to you."

As George Frideric left the church, he was stopped by freckle-faced Herman Mann. "And what will you do with that book?" he demanded.

"I want to know everything about music."

Herman shrugged. "The only reason I'm taking lessons is because of Papa. He thinks it will improve my life. Fish whiskers! I hate music lessons."

Again and again Herman, or the twins, Helmet and Hans, tried to persuade George Frideric to go fishing. But he wasn't interested. "I want to learn all the music I can," he said.

"Why?" Hans screwed his face into a knot.

"Because music makes people happy. Also—" He hesitated. "Also, I know that God wants me to be a musician."

"How do you know that?"

"Because He has filled my heart with a love for music. I love an organ and I'd rather play one than go fishing."

The week of lessons went by quickly and soon it was Sunday. George Frideric awoke with anticipation. He hoped he could sit near the front of the church so he could study the techniques of Herr Zachow as he squeezed the best possible music out of the organ.

Quickly he donned his Sunday clothes. He was combing his hair when he remembered the note his mother had pinned to the clothes he took to Weissenfels. Where was it?

At Weissenfels, he had placed the note in the right pocket of his britches. He distinctly remembered that. Now, he searched in all his pockets, but the note was missing. Could Anna have taken it?

Having made certain that no one was listening, he faced his aunt. "Did you take that note out of my pocket?" he asked.

"No, I ironed your suit; but the pockets were all empty. I remember the occasion very well."

"Maybe Father found it," said George Frideric, "and if he did he may think that we tricked him."

Anna's face turned a shade whiter and she covered her mouth with her palm. "Let's hope not," she said.

At the breakfast table, George Handel seemed unusually talkative. "Well, I guess the son of my old age is going to be a musician,'' he said as he spread a coat of butter over his bread. ''That makes everyone happy but me. This week I heard about an unusual lawsuit. It was all about a will.'' He took a bite of bread, focused his eyes on George Frideric, and continued.

''When the lawyer who was out to break the will faced the jury, he did not make a speech. Instead, he had a single question: 'You are farmers,' he said. 'Now I want to know one thing. When your plow crosses a narrow ditch, does it go down into the ditch, or over the ditch?' He then sat down.

''Later, at the proper moment, he had each member of the jury study the will through a magnifying glass. As they studied it, they discovered a break in the writing when it crossed the crease where it had been folded.

'''Why are those words broken?' he asked. 'They are broken because they were written across the fold of the will a long time after the deceased had written the will. Someone has altered this will.'

''That was the end of the lawsuit. The will was read as it was originally written and the rightful heirs received their lawful portion of the estate. As I thought about this case, I pictured George Frideric in that lawyer's place. Something inside of me assures me that George Frideric could be a great lawyer. In time, he might even plead a case before the emperor.

''Ah, but that's not to be.'' He sighed and slowly spread a dab of jelly over the remainder of his bread. Then as a cloud covered his face, he concluded, ''It is indeed remarkable what the study of a bit of paper can reveal.''

A frozen silence followed that statement.

George Frideric was staring at his plate when he felt a touch on his elbow. Looking down, he faced

Petrina who was again heavy with kittens. "You're always begging," he chided. "Well, here's a bit of sausage for your majesty."

As George Frideric accompanied his father to the church, he wondered if he would have to sit in the rear. But no, his father led him and his sister to their regular pew just behind the organ. While watching Zachow's nimble feet and fingers, he could not restrain from imitating him on the pew directly in front. He tried to concentrate on the sermon which was on the genealogy of Jesus. But he could not. Instead, his mind kept wondering whether Papa had found the note.

During his second year with Zachow, George Handel turned to George Frideric while he was relaxing in the living room. "Tell me, son," he said, "what is the meaning of harmony?"

"Harmony is the study of chords."

"Chords?"

"Yes, two or more tones when sounded together make harmony. Zachow is teaching me which tones are pleasant when sounded together and which are not. He is also teaching me which set of tones should follow another set. It's all very difficult, for the chords must fit in with the melody."

Handel laughed. "I can understand human anatomy. But I can't understand chords."

"That's because you are a surgeon."

"True. But I'm curious. Now explain to me the meaning of counterpoint."

"Counterpoint is two or more melodies woven together. It used to be called *polyphony*. *Poly* means many and *phony* means voices. When great cathedrals and large choirs came into being, musicians began to use counterpoint. The tunes have to be woven in such a way that they do not clash."

George Handel shook his head. "How do you know all that?"

"Study."

"It seems to me that producing great music is terribly difficult, especially for the composer."

"Yes, Papa, it is. The melody itself, like the song of a bird is easy. It's the weaving in of the chords and counterpoint that's hard. But, Papa, there's nothing in this world that I love as much as I love music. I would rather have my hands cut off than not to be a musician."

During George Frideric's third year of study under Zachow, the organist said, "You must learn to play other instruments besides the organ."

"Why?"

"So you will know how to harmonize them together."

As George Frideric learned to play the violin and other instruments, Herr Zachow insisted that he compose music for an entire church service each week. "This is a lot of work," he explained. "But it will teach you to compose quickly. Scarlatti often composes an entire opera in a week or two."

Thinking of a melody and arranging chords and counterpoint was hard. But George Frideric didn't mind. The notes to him were like soldiers in an army; and he, the general, was privileged to determine their neighbors, the length of their appearance, and the speed of the procession.

When he was eleven, George Frideric knew that he had learned all that Herr Zachow could teach him. Zachow also knew this. But where was George Frideric to go for advanced training? He confided his problem to both his mother and Aunt Anna. Each of them assured him that they would ask the Lord to open a way for him.

Petrina had another litter of kittens and then another. The last litter was her largest. Of the seven, three were black, one was yellow, and three were white with black spots. Often as George Frideric worked on his school lessons or was in deep thought about music, Petrina would lead her kittens into the room, wash their faces, and stretch out as they had their breakfast.

One morning George Frideric found that one of the black kittens had died. He took it outside, buried it; and placed a marker so he could remember its grave. When he returned to the house he found Petrina was grieving. Uttering deep-throated meows, she searched in each corner, in the closet, under the table, in the bedrooms. He felt sorry for her. Then, all at once, her mood changed. She dismissed her sorrow, returned to her remaining kittens, scrubbed them some more, purred, and entertained them by twitching her tail.

"Do you think Petrina is teaching us a lesson?" Asked George Frideric at the table while the family was having lunch.

"Of course," replied his mother.

Three months after Petrina had lost her kitten, George Handel strode into the house in such a hurry Dorothea stared. "Are the police after you?" she asked.

"No, the police are not after me; but I received a letter that will change all of our lives. Summon the family. It is important that we discuss this together."

"What's it about?" asked George Frideric as a cold fear began to twist his insides.

"You'll learn that when the family has assembled."

"Can't you give me a hint?"

"In a moment."

6

Berlin

As the family assembled in the living room, George Frideric strained not to show the anxiety that was twisting his insides. He felt even more desperate than he had felt when he was perched in the tree and the ants and all their friends were feasting on him. Between his speeded breaths, he kept asking himself: *What does Papa want? Has he found an excuse to stop my music study?*

Clad in his usual surgeon's black, and with his long white hair slightly askew, George Handel was in an excitable mood when he strode into the room. Following a nervous cough, he announced, "Our family has been highly honored. During my more than seventy years I've talked to generals, dukes, and even princes. But this morning I received a letter from Berlin." He withdrew it from his coat pocket. "This letter," he began with a quiver in his voice, "was written by Sophia Charlotte. Think of it. A letter addressed to me, a humble surgeon in Halle, by Sophia Charlotte."

"Who is Sophia Charlotte?" asked George Frideric.

He spoke before he realized the depreciating effect of
his question.

"Sophia Charlotte is the wife of the future king of
Germany, and a descendent of English kings. Her
great-grandfather was James I, who ordered an
English translation of the Bible in 1611."

"And what does Sophia Charlotte want from us?"
asked Dorothea.

"She wants our son, George Frideric, to go to
Berlin and play the clavichord in her court." His voice
rang with pride.

"And are you going to let him go?"

"Berlin is a long, long way northeast of here. It's
at least one hundred miles. That means a journey of
nearly a week by stage."

"Are you going to let him go?"

George Handel ran his palms down his long hair,
smoothing it out. Then he thoughtfully licked his lips.
Finally he said, "What do you think about it?"

George Frideric held his breath as he watched this
drama. Herr Zachow had told him about how Berlin
was becoming a musical center. If the way were
opened for him to go, he could meet some of the
greatest musicians in the world. As he awaited the
verdict, Petrina majestically led in her newest
squadron of kittens, along with the orphan kittens
from next door. She selected a place on the rug and
invited the kittens—the entire colony—to lunch.

"I think it's in the Lord's will for him to go,"
ventured Dorothea. She spoke in a low voice.

"And so do I," added Dorothea Sophia, shaking
her pigtails.

"Maybe my vote doesn't count," put in Anna.
"But I think God has answered my prayers and
worked a miracle. I believe he should go." She spoke
with enthusiasm.

"And what about you, Johanna Christina?" asked George Handel.

"I'll miss him," she answered, her bright eyes shining. "But I think he should go. Now you should ask Petrina."

"And what do you say, Petrina?" asked Handel, suppressing a smile.

Petrina's only response was to wink an eye and yawn.

"That means she's neutral," decreed Handel. He spoke in the same tone of voice he used when advising a patient.

"How about me?" asked George Frideric playfully.

"Oh, we already know what your vote is," replied his father. "Actually, however, none of your votes were needed. This may surprise you, but I've already made the arrangements. You will leave next Thursday. I'm mighty proud of you. You have brought honor to the family."

George Frideric was so stunned he couldn't reply. The only one who wasn't shaken was Petrina. Upon hearing the news, she got up, stretched, yawned, and walked off. She took her lunch counter with her. The kittens followed.

The next day the Lutheran Gymnasium was buzzing with the fame that had come to Halle even before George Frideric took his seat. Since the intense excitement made schoolwork impossible, the teacher finally said, "Halle has been highly honored by the request of Sophia Charlotte for our own George Frideric Handel to go to Berlin and play for her and others in the royal palace. As you know, she's the wife of an elector. Thus, she's an electress." He selected a fresh piece of chalk. "Since we've been studying history, you may have a few questions."

George Frideric pushed up his hand. "Please

explain the meaning of an elector.''

The teacher smiled. ''That's an excellent request. All of you know that we live in Germany. But you should also know that Germany is part of the Holy Roman Empire. Electors are archbishops, kings, and rulers in nine provinces of the empire.''

The teacher sketched on the blackboard an outline of the empire and its provinces.

''When an emperor dies,'' he continued, ''the electors meet to choose a new one. If they don't make a decision within thirty days, they are required to live on bread and water until they name their man. Electors have a lot of power. Each can say to a candidate, if you want my vote, you will have to make some concessions. Such bargains have changed the maps of Europe. In addition to favors the candidates are required to pay the electors huge sums of money. This means that next to the emperor, electors are the most powerful men on earth.''

''Does this mean that George Frideric will be performing before one the most important people on earth?'' asked Herman Mann.

''It does.''

''Fish whiskers! I'd rather stay in Halle and fish,'' said Herman.

A boy across the aisle whispered, ''Don't be jealous.''

Except for the trip with his father to Weissenfels, George Frideric had never been away from home. As he scrunched near the outside window of the stagecoach, his eyes fastened on his parents, sisters, and Aunt Anna, it was difficult for him to believe that he was headed for Berlin and would soon be playing the clavichord in a palace.

The coachman hoisted himself onto his seat, flicked

the reins, and they were off. George Frideric waved
his handkerchief to the family until, because of a
sudden turn, he could no longer see them.

As the coach gathered speed, a flow of tears washed
his cheeks. When at last he gained control, he examined the packages his parents had given him. His
mother's contained a Bible and a note which read,
"When in trouble turn to Philippians 1:21." His
father's gift was a small leather bag filled with coins
and a folded note. The note, written in his father's
scrawl, stated: "I'm mighty proud of the son of my
old age." When he turned it over, he stared. Then
another flood of tears blinded his eyes.

Yes, his father had written those words on the other
side of the note his mother had pinned to his Sunday
suit when he went to Weissenfels. *Could it be that his
father had discouraged him from studying music because he
knew that would inspire him to work harder to become a
musician?* Perhaps!

On the second day of the journey, an elderly man
with one leg and a heavy notebook under his arm,
squeezed awkwardly onto the seat next to George
Frideric. "Hope my wooden leg doesn't bother you,"
he wheezed. "Lost my leg in the Thirty Years' War."

"The Thirty Years' War?" George Frideric was
intrigued.

"Yes, the Thirty Years' War. Started in 1618.
Ended in 1648. It was the bloodiest war ever fought,
and like all wars it accomplished nothing but to fill
graves—thousands and thousands of graves." He
stroked his carefully trimmed full beard which was
slightly darker than his thinning cotton-white hair.
"I'm writing a book about that war." He stared out
the window at a herd of cattle. Then after a long
moment, he broke his silence. "Each war gets bloodier
than the last."

"Why is that?" asked George Frideric.

"Better guns." The man twitched his right cheek.

"And what caused the Thirty Years' War?"

"It started as a religious war." The one-legged man stroked his beard again, and then launched into a long story of Protestants fighting Catholics, and of rulers hating each other. He continued over soup at an inn while fresh horses were being harnessed to the stagecoach. And with his rapt audience of one, he continued during the rest of the day's trip.

"Why did the people hate each other?" George Frideric asked at one point in the story. "After all, both sides read the same Bible and all of them believed in Jesus Christ."

"Why?"

"Because of the doctrine, especially the one which concerns the elements used in the Lord's Supper." The white head shook with his own disbelief. "That war should never have been fought."

George Frideric learned more history than he had ever learned in school. On the third day of the trip he asked, "Is there some way the Christians with differing doctrinal beliefs could work together? Just think of the influence they would have if they could."

The writer shrugged. "Do you have anything in mind?"

"Maybe it could be done with music. All Christians believe in Jesus, the Resurrection, the Ascension, the Second Coming."

"Ah, but Protestants wouldn't be happy with the images in Catholic churches; and Catholics wouldn't be happy with married priests; and the Calvinists wouldn't be happy with Lutheran hymns; and the Anabaptists wouldn't like stained windows." He stroked his beard.

George Frideric smiled. "Perhaps there's another way. Maybe different types of Christians could be inspired by great music played in a neutral place."

"Like a theater?"

"Well, maybe not a theater. Some theaters are associated with too much evil. But how about concert halls?"

"Mmmmm. You may be right."

At the end of the fourth day, the writer said, "Well here's where I get off. It's strange, but we haven't introduced ourselves. I'm Professor Otto Kramer. And you?"

"George Frideric Handel."

"Are you the son of George Handel, the surgeon from Halle?"

"I am."

"I know about your father. He's the one who pulled a dagger out of a boy's abdomen. And I know about the city of Halle. It was where I lost my leg. We put too much powder in our cannon and it blew up."

At 11 a. m. on the fifth day, the coachman barked, "We'll be in Berlin in one hour. That will be the end of our trip."

To George Frideric, those last minutes seemed like hours. Speaking to a plump lady encased in a floor-length gown, he asked, "Do you know much about Berlin?"

"I've lived there nine years."

"What's the population?"

"About twenty thousand."

George Frideric gasped. "I c-can't imagine that many people. Do you ever get lost?"

The lady held up a jeweled hand and laughed. "It's not *that* big. If you'll tell me where you'll be staying, maybe I can tell you how to get there."

"I'll be a guest of Sophia Charlotte."

"Sophia Charlotte!" Her eyes widened. Then she added, "You must be a musician. She invites all the great musicians to the palace. If you're her guest, she'll have a coachman to meet you."

The mention of Sophia Charlotte stopped the buzz of conversation and each eye riveted on George Frideric. Squirming under their gaze, he remained silent and stared out the window. Soon, they entered the city. From his viewpoint, he noticed muddy streets, thatched houses, and pigs rooting at the base of rows of lime trees along the street.

Presently the stagecoach slid to a stop and a man dressed in a crimson uniform came to the door. "I'm looking for Herr George Frideric Handel," he announced.

7

Problems

As the crimson-suited coachman guided white horses down the streets of Berlin, George Frideric tingled with excitement. He was in a fantastic new world. Not only was the coach brilliant with gold leaf, but the seats were soft and covered with beautiful velvet. More startling yet, each time the coach passed in front of a person, that person bowed low, and if it was a man, doffed his cap.

"You will be staying with some other musicians," said the coachman after he had taken George Frideric's luggage to the door of a fine hotel whose main door was guarded by huge marble lions. "Dinner will be served at the palace at eight. If you feel famished between now and then, summon a waiter. Order anything you like. I'll return in time to take you and the other musicians to the palace."

Before stretching out on the bed in the room to which the clerk had led him, George Frideric checked his watch with the clock over the main desk. Then he tried to sleep. But sleep eluded him. There were so many things to see: the excellent paintings on the wall, the enameled pitcher and basin on the stand in the corner, the heavy rug, the fluttering curtains, the hunting scene on the tapestry behind his bed. Suddenly, however, a deep sleep caught up with him.

After what seemed like a very short nap, George Frideric was awakened by the clerk's sharp rap at the door. "The coach will be here in half an hour," said the man. George Frideric quickly freshened his face, changed his clothes, and made his way over to the front desk. As he awaited the coach, he said to the desk clerk, "Please, sir, maybe you can help me. I-I've n-n-never seen an Electress. H-how s-s-should I-I address her?"

"No need to worry," assured the clerk. "Electress Charlotte is very understanding. She adores musicians. Address her with the words, Your Highness."

"Does she know anything about music?"

"Of course. She's always heard good music in the palace; and she took lessons on the harpsichord. I've heard her play."

"Tell me, how am I supposed to eat? I-I've never eaten with such important people before."

The clerk laughed. "Don't worry. Keep your eye on the Electress and do whatever she does. I've never eaten with her. But that's what I'd do if I were in your place."

The coach was so jammed with musicians, George Frideric was barely able to wedge himself between a plump violinist and an even fatter trumpeter. As the coach bumped along, George Frideric listened to conversations between the musicians.

"A month ago I was in Venice," said the violinist. "Marvelous city. It's made up of a hundred-twenty tiny islands, and it has canals instead of streets. People move from place to place by means of gondolas.

Shaped like narrow melon rinds, those little boats can carry from a half dozen to a dozen passengers. The boatmen move them with long paddles and poles which they push to the sides or bottoms of the canals. I had a wonderful time. I even got to hear Allesandro Scarlatti.''

"What's he like?'' interrupted George Frideric, unable to contain himself.

"He's great. Can play anything. His greatest talents are composing and conducting operas. Operas leap from his fingers like water from a fountain. I went to *Teodora* three times!'' The violinist shook his head.

Other musicians joined in the conversation, and George Frideric listened as they described the aqueducts and fountains of Rome, the smoke and flame that billowed from Vesuvius, the marvels of Florence, the sculptures of Michelangelo, the remains of the Appian Way, the dome of St. Peter's, and the marvelous operas in which they had participated.

Presently the coach stopped at the gates of the palace. There, George Frideric followed the other musicians as they passed the armed guards standing in frozen attention before each of the doors.

The long table at which George Frideric was seated was crowded with guests, musicians, palace officials, members of the nobility. The Electress and her husband sat across from him.

Artificial light was provided by huge crystal chandeliers in which fingers of candles trembled from a breath of air seeping through the tall, slightly ajar stained glass windows at the rear of the enormous dining room. Other candles clamped in ornate receptacles on the walls completed the lighting system.

George Frideric's eyes widened at the sight of so much food. Each of three platters on each table contained a small but complete roasted pig with an ear of corn in its mouth; several plates were loaded with enormous pike and similar fish; and there were wide plates brimming with baked quail and other fowl. In addition, nestled amidst vases of flowers, there were two wooden trenchers heaped with roast beef, joints of mutton, slabs of ham, lengths of sausage. Also, there were many steaming bowls of vegetables. And besides these staples there were pies, jams, bowls of fruit, and pitchers of drinks filled with chunks of ice.

As the guests waited, the Electress asked the chaplain to lead in prayer, then she began to eat. Her first bite was a signal for the guests to make selections and begin to eat. While those around him gorged, slurped, belched, and refilled their plates, George Frideric kept his eyes on the Electress. When she cut a piece of beef, he cut a piece of beef; when she drank, he drank. Then, after eating a bit of pike, she reached for the milk and filled a saucer with it. Although puzzled about the reason for this maneuvre, George Frideric did the same.

A moment later, the Electress pushed back her chair, placed her milk-filled saucer on the floor, and summoned the cat. Embarrassed, George Frideric stared at the saucer he had just filled. Soon others were staring and he was wishing he could disappear. In spite of trying, he had entertained everyone by doing the wrong thing. Nonetheless, he, too, placed the saucer on the floor.

Conscious that his ears were red, George Frideric pushed his seat back and tried to eat. But it was impossible to take a single bite, for everyone was laughing.

"That's all right," said the Electress' husband Ernest Augustus, after he had calmed the laughter by lifting his hand. "Puss just had eight kittens and she can use another saucer of milk."

Wishing that he could disappear, George Frideric's appetite vanished. As he was picking at his food and forcing his jaws to chew, the Electress stood. "This evening," she said, "we are privileged to have with us one of the greatest musicians in all of Germany. He is still in his youth. But he is as talented as any of the Bachs. George Frideric Handel has not been warned that he would play for us tonight. But from what I've learned, he's always ready. Our young guest, the son of Halle's great surgeon George Handel, will now step over to our clavichord and play for us."

Although completely unprepared, George Frideric managed to get over to the clavichord, an instrument he had not seen until that moment. As he searched his mind for what he should play, a silent voice seemed to say, *play the hymns of Dr. Martin Luther*. But should he? Those hymns were for church. This was a banquet. As he wrestled with the problem, he carefully adjusted himself on the bench and prayed for guidance. Again, the silent voice said, *play the hymns of Dr. Martin Luther*.

Assured that he was being led by the Lord, George Frideric played *A Mighty Fortress*. He used all the skill he possessed. Then he went on with several other of the reformer's hymns and concluded with his *Away in a Manger*. When he stood and bowed he was met with thunderous applause and the guests kept clapping for an encore.

"I'm sorry," said George Frideric, "I did not come prepared to play tonight. My music is at the hotel."

"Repeat something," shouted a voice.

"What?"

"*A Mighty Fortress*."

"Aren't you tired of it?"

"No."

George Frideric hesitated. While he pondered, a man with only one eye and one arm made his way forward. "You must repeat it," he said. His voice was husky with deep emotion. "That hymn is called the Battle Hymn of the Reformation, and so it is. I'm a veteran of the Thirty Years' War. It was that hymn that kept our chins up. It helped us keep going when we were out of food and were outnumbered ten to one."

Returning to the clavichord, George Frideric was about to start when the Electress stood. "On the last verse," she said, "we will all stand and sing that mighty hymn together."

After the singing, George Frideric went back to his place at the table. His appetite had returned. He finished everything on his plate, then he filled it again with ham, fish, beef, and huge slices of bread. After these things had disappeared, he helped himself to the fruit and cut a large wedge of pie.

The next morning George Frideric discovered that he was a celebrity. Even the hotel clerks treated him with a mysterious awe. He became a guest at a banquet almost every night. He played various instruments at crowded halls; gave concerts on the church organ; and was always seated next to the Electress. By the end of the month he had been dubbed "The Celebrated Saxon," the name referring to Saxony, the area of Germany where he lived.

At breakfast toward the end of his fifth week in Berlin, a messenger in crimson livery handed him an envelope. It was an invitation from the Electress and her husband for him to dine with them in a private meeting at the palace.

After a sumptuous meal which ended with caviar, Prince Ernest Augustus turned to George Frideric. "The Electress and I are impressed with your talent," said the future king of Germany. "You have an almost magic touch. Both of us feel that you should make a trip to Italy. There, you would meet some of the world's great musicians, including Allesandro Scarlatti." The Prince, magnificently attired in his resplendent uniform, leaned forward. "Does that appeal to you?" he asked.

"It does," replied George Frideric. "But trips like that cost lots of money. Where—"

"Money will be no problem. The Electress and I will supply it. You will stay at fine hotels, meet important people, and play in the great concert halls in Venice, Rome, Naples, Florence, and other cities."

"I'm overwhelmed," replied George Frideric. He made an effort to calm the quiver in his voice. "B-but I w-wouldn-t w-w-w-want to go on such a trip without Father's permission."

"I'm glad to hear that," replied the Prince. "Neither the Electress nor I would want you to disobey him in this matter. And because of that I've already written to him."

"You've already written?"

"Yes, I've already written to him. Sent the letter on Monday."

That night George Frideric was farther from sleep than he had ever been. It seemed to him that the gates of paradise were flung wide open and that Gabriel was pointing the way to the Throne. Before him was an exciting trip across the Alps, and visits to Rome, Venice, Florence, Naples, and perhaps even a visit with Allesandro Scarlatti.

Ah, but what would he do if his father refused permission?

Hours and then days and then weeks crept by without an answer from Halle. George Frideric kept busy. He attended concerts and was featured in concerts. He queried other musicians about techniques.

He went on short trips. He ate at expensive restaurants. Each time he met the Electress he inquired if she had heard from his father. But each time her answer was a negative shake of her head. Soon he began to wonder if one of the letters had been lost in the mail. Then, at the end of a busy week, he was summoned to the palace.

"We received a letter from your father this week," said the Prince.

"Yes?" questioned George Frideric eagerly.

"The answer is no. Your father wants you to return to Halle and enter the university."

Although he had braced himself, George Frideric visibly shuddered. He felt as if he had been struck in the solar plexus with brass knuckles. While wiping his eyes, he said, "I'm deeply disappointed."

"We could use our influence to persuade him to change his mind," offered the Prince. "Still, he's your father. If you want us to write, let us know. Go to your hotel and pray about it."

"Yes, Your Highness, that's what I'll do."

George Frideric threw himself across the bed and sobbed. His entire world had come to an end. Then he fumbled for the Bible his mother had given him. As he searched for it, he came to her note which stated, "When in trouble, turn to Philippians 1:21." Having neglected his Bible, he had to use the index to find that passage. After locating it, he read: "For me to live is Christ, and to die is gain." He swallowed hard as he contemplated that. Yes, those words were true. *But was he to miss the opportunity of a lifetime because of one of his father's moods?*

Sobbing, and then pacing the floor, George Frideric prayed for guidance. Then he went back to his Bible. The pages fell open to Ephesians 6:1, one of his father's favorite passages. There he read: "Children,

obey your parents in the Lord: for this is right.''
Angrily, he snapped the Bible shut, went to the dining
room, and ordered a bowl of soup. Then he went for
a long walk.

Praying as he walked, George Frideric was convinced that the Apostle Paul was right. He should obey
his father. That evening he went to the palace.

"Your Highness," he said as he addressed the
Electress, "I am convinced that I should obey my
father. But I want to thank you and the Prince for
your gracious offer.''

The Electress studied him silently for a long
moment. Then she asked, "How old are you?''

"I'm going on twelve.''

"Mmmmm. Mmmmm.'' The Electress
thoughtfully rubbed her chin. "Well, you have your
whole life ahead of you. You are doing right by obey-
ing your father. Other doors will open.'' Her face
suddenly brightened. "I shall write to my brother
George Ludwig in Hanover this very afternoon.
George loves music and when you've completed your
courses at the university, you might be able to work
with him.'' She then handed him a small bag filled
with gold coins. "Use this money to buy something
you really need.''

"Yes, Your Highness, I will do just that.''

As George Frideric packed his suitcase, he felt a
lump in his throat. *Would he ever again have such an
opportunity to visit Italy?* At the same time he felt an
assurance that he was being guided by the Heavenly
Father.

8
Halle

George Frideric's mother was waiting at the depot when his coach arrived. On the way home, she said, "George and I are excited about the unbelievable things that have been happening to you. We're proud that you're our son. But—" She lowered her voice. "But, I'm glad you're back. Papa isn't a bit well. If—" She dabbed at her eyes and her voice became husky, "if the good Lord doesn't perform a miracle he won't be with us long. Papa is pleased you didn't go to Italy."

The moment he entered their house, George Frideric mounted the steps to his parents' bedroom. He peered into his father's wasted face and shuddered. His cheeks and eye sockets resembled those of an ancient skull; and his arms were so withered they seemed like sections of kindling.

"I've returned to attend school," announced George Frideric.

"A wise decision. You're only young once."

"I agree. I'll return to the Lutheran Gymnasium

and prepare for the University of Halle.''

''Great! And I hope you'll study law. I want you to be a success. I'm proud of the way you stormed Berlin. Still—'' He shook his head and combed his long cotton-white hair with his fingers. ''Still, there's no future in music. But, of course, if God has called you to be a musician, that's different.''

Each day after school George Frideric hurried to his father's room and read to him from the Bible. The sinking man's favorite passages were about the birth, ministry, and death of Jesus. He especially loved the passion scenes in the Gospel according to John. Then quite by accident, George Frideric turned to Revelation 19:6. Thinking his father might like that passage, he read:

> And I heard as it were the voice of a great multitude, and as the voice of many waters, and as the voice of mighty thunderings, saying Alleluia: for the Lord God omnipotent reigneth.

''Son, read that last sentence again,'' said Handel with deep emotion. ''And read it slowly.''

> The . . . Lord . . . God . . . omnipotent . . . reigneth.

''Now read it again,'' ordered the old man, his eyes lighting up.

After George Frideric had read it the fifth time, his father said, ''Those words, my son, are true. God rules. I lived through part of the Thirty Years' War. I lost my wife and children during the plague, and eight years ago I nearly died. But I believe God rules and God has a purpose in everything. Yes, everything!''

Following that long speech, George Handel sank even lower in the bed. He was utterly exhausted.

That winter George Frideric's father died at the age

of seventy-five. One of many paragraphs eventually inscribed on his tombstone read:

> In true faith in God and in the precious merits of his redeemer, Jesus Christ, [he] fell asleep on 11th Feb. 1697, and his body rests here till the joyful resurrection of all believers.

Following the funeral, the sermon along with several "mourning" poems, were printed in a small booklet. One of the poems was composed by George Frideric. This was his first work to ever appear in print. The lines hint at his thoughts and his plans for the future.

> Ah! bitter grief! my dearest father's heart
> From me by cruel death is torn away.
> Ah! misery! and ah! the bitter smart
> Which seizes me, poor orphan from this day.
>
> God, who bereaves me of a father's care
> By that dear father's death, yet liveth still;
> And henceforth, in mine anguish and despair,
> I find my help and guidance in His Will.

The lines indicate that the twelve-year-old had a fine sense of rhythm and drama. He signed it, George Frideric Handel, "dedicated to the liberal arts."

Left without her husband's considerable medical income, Dorothea Handel arranged for her home to be divided into two apartments. She lived in one and rented the other. This income plus the payments received from the sale of the medical practice enabled her to remain in Halle at a reduced standard of living.

During the turmoil of remodeling, Petrina disappeared. "Where do you think she's gone?" inquired George Frideric.

"Cats often move when the world they've known changes," replied Anna.

"I hope she isn't dead."

"If she is—" Anna smiled. "If her life has ended, she still accomplished more than most people. Her kittens are all over Halle and they're doing a good job of ridding the city of rats. Petrina has left her mark in the world."

Strongly motivated, George Frideric worked hard at the Lutheran Gymnasium. He even fell in love with Latin. Halle became a city of culture. Famous musicians filled the concert halls; Shakespeare's plays were featured; and the events of the world were discussed by those inclined to learn. Rapid changes were taking place. George Frideric followed them with interest. The word *why* was constantly on his tongue.

China conquered western Mongolia; the French attempted to colonize West Africa; Peter, a near seven-foot giant who ruled Russia, visited Germany, Holland, England and Austria in order to gain information so he could westernize Russia. He took back to Russia the western calendar, so the year there suddenly changed from 7208 to 1700.

While these sensational things were going on, George Frideric was busy at school. On February 10, 1702, at the age of seventeen, he enrolled at the University of Halle.

He did not register as a law student.

Money was a problem. Dorothea Handel often had difficulty in paying her ordinary household bills. "How are you going to meet your expenses?" asked a friend as they approached the library.

"I-I don't know," confessed Handel. He stepped off the graveled path in order to miss a series of puddles. "But I feel an assurance that if I follow the directions of the Lord He will supply all my needs."

One of Handel's professors was August Hermann Francke, a zealous man who was a Pietist. He taught that although Christians are saved by faith alone, their faith should be accompanied by good works. And, to prove that he believed what he taught, Francke operated an orphanage at nearby Glauchau. Handel often went with this professor of Greek, Oriental languages, and theology to his orphanage.

"You see that lad?" asked Francke, pointing to a boy behind a desk in a corner. "He was forsaken by his parents and so we brought him here. He's doing well. He may even enter the university later on. And look over there, that little girl was found in a rubbish heap. But we rescued her." He then placed a hand on George Frideric's shoulder. "Why don't you play something for them?"

After a couple of boys had gone outside to work the bellows, Handel gave a short concert. The children clapped and stomped and demanded more. "I wish we could stay," said Professor Francke at last, "but we must get back to Halle."

At the door, a boy on crutches held Handel's hand. "You inspired me," he said. "I, too, want to be an organist."

As they were leaving for Halle, Handel leaned across the carriage. "Who was that who said he wanted to be an organist?"

"Oh, that's Hans Gottleib. His parents' home was burned down. They are utterly destitute. He was crippled by disease."

"Does he have any talent?"

"I'm sure he does. He often plays in morning chapel."

"I do wish I could help him," said George Frideric.

"Perhaps the time will come when you can." Francke withdrew a New Testament from his pocket. "Helping others is our mission in life. Listen to these words of Jesus: 'For I was an hungered, and ye gave me meat: I was a stranger, and ye took me in: naked and ye clothed me: I was sick and ye visited me: I was in prison and ye came unto me. Then shall the righteous answer him, saying, Lord, when saw we thee hungered, and fed thee? or thirsty, and gave thee drink?

" 'When saw we thee a stranger, and took thee in? or naked, and clothed thee? Or when saw we thee sick, or in prison, and came unto thee?

" 'And the King shall answer and say unto them, Verily I say unto you, Inasmuch as ye have done it unto one of the least of these my brethren, ye have done it unto me' (Matt. 25:35-40)."

Francke closed his New Testament and thrust it back into his pocket. "Those words of Jesus have been forgotten by far too many," he said.

"Herr Francke," asked George Frideric thoughtfully, " Does your salvation depend upon your work with the orphans?"

"Certainly not! But my increased joy does. I'm never as happy as I am when I'm with my orphans. Working with them stimulates my mind."

For the next several days the scenes at the orphanage and the glow in Hans Gottleib's eyes dominated George Frideric's thinking. He wished he could do something to help those orphans. But he was mired down in his own problems. His tuition would soon be due and he had no money, nor did his mother. As the day his tuition money was required drew near, he went into his room, closed the door, knelt by his bed, and turned the matter over to the Lord.

Within a few weeks of his enrollment at the university, Handel was stopped by an officer of the Calvinist Church known as the Dom-Kirche.

"Would you play the organ for us next Sunday?" asked the man.

"I would be glad to," replied Handel. "But remember I'm a Lutheran."

"That doesn't make any difference," replied the stubby man. "You are a Christian and that's what really matters."

The organ at the Dom-Kirche was not as large as the one at Our Lady's Church; but George Frideric soon got used to it and made it produce more music than it had ever produced before. After the service, many of the members thronged around him. "We wish you could be our regular organist," said an officer from the bank. "You have a marvelous touch."

Later in the week, George Frideric was summoned to a committee meeting at the Dom-Kirche. He had a good idea about what would be discussed even before he arrived. This is because he had heard several whiffs of gossip about their regular organist. The man was drinking and carousing so much he frequently did not show up for the services.

"We would like for you to become our regular organist," said the leader of the committee as he peered over the top of his gold-rimmed glasses into Handel's face. He nervously coughed into a wide handkerchief. "Would you consider that position?"

"Certainly. But you must keep in mind that I'm only eighteen and that I want to remain a Lutheran."

"That's all right," replied the leader. "Martin Luther and John Calvin were good friends and both of them taught that 'the just shall live by faith'." He then turned to the other members of the group. "Perhaps you have some questions you'd like to ask."

"Have you ever been drunk?" asked a tiny man with huge eyes.

"Certainly not!"

"Are you going to be married soon?" asked another.

"No. I haven't even thought about it."

"Do *you* have any questions?" asked the leader, addressing Handel.

"Yes, I have one question. Will I be allowed to continue at the university?"

"Of course," replied several, speaking almost in unison.

George Frideric's appointment as the official organist at the Dom-Kirche was set down in writing on March 13, 1702. The last paragraph of the agreement read:

> In return for his trouble and performance he is promised and assigned as a stipend for the probationary year . . . fifty thalers, which he will draw from the Royal Purse of this province . . . in quarterly instalments of 12 thalers 12 gulden, beginning next Trinity Sunday, and in addition free lodging in the Moritzburg most generally assigned to organists by His Royal Highness.
>
> "This appointment is given at Halle under the hands and seals of us, the Pastors and Elders . . . "

George Frideric's financial problems were solved. Moreover, now that he had a room of his own, his mother had an extra one which she might rent.

Yes, the words of Revelation 19:6 were true. Inspired by the comment of his father when he read them at his bedside, George Frideric opened his New Testament and reread them:

> And I heard as it were the voice of a great multitude, and as the voice of many waters, and as the voice of mighty thunderings, saying Alleluia: for the Lord God omnipotent reigneth.

9

Saved
By A Button

Rushing from classes to the Dom-Kirche for Sunday services or organ practice kept Handel busy. Still, he enjoyed split-second activity. Many students at the university wasted their time at cards, drinking, gambling, carousing, and even fighting duels. Not Handel. He had decided that his life would count and he had no time for trivia.

Life at the university was interesting. New ideas were constantly being presented and the world was rapidly changing. In 1701 the husband of Sophia Charlotte became King Fredrick I of Germany, and he began to make Germany a military state. The next year, Queen Anne came to the British throne. Anne was Protestant and spent her reign firming the *Glorious Revolution* started by her predecessor. This was a bloodless revolution in which England became officially Protestant.

Such political events inspired discussion and,

sometimes, angry debates among the students. Across a restaurant table, a student confronted Handel.

"Have you heard about Peter's latest idea of raising taxes in Russia?" he asked.

"No." Handel concentrated on working out the bones in a section of fish.

"He's decreed that all official papers—receipts, contracts, petitions, an so on—have to be written on a special paper bearing the government's symbol of an eagle. That paper, of course, is taxed. Receipts written on ordinary paper have no value."

Handel chuckled. "That's nothing," he said. "Vespasian taxed toilets throughout the Roman Empire. In time some bright king will tax wigs and then windows." He thoughtfully chewed the last piece of fish. "But I must hurry. Have an examination in British history."

"Before you go," cut in another student, "I must tell you something else the old boy is doing. Since he visited the West, Peter decided he doesn't like the long robes the Russians were wearing. At an elaborate banquet, he snipped off the sleeves of the man sitting next to him. Cut 'em off just below the elbow. 'See,' he explained, 'these things are in your way. They upset glasses and sometimes they fall into the sauce.' He then handed the sleeves to the man and said, 'Make gaiters out of them.'

"But that didn't satisfy Peter. Oh, no. Now he's stationed guards at the gates leading into Moscow. Anyone who passes through the gates is required to kneel on the street. Then the guard cuts off his robe where it touches the cobblestones."

While everyone was laughing, Handel started for the door. Hand on knob, he said, "Some of us in the West also need to make some changes."

"Like what?" demanded the one who had told about robes in Russia.

"We could start with music. Even church music needs more life. We have such glorious things to sing about: the Resurrection, the Atonement, the Ascension, the drama in the Old Testament. And yet—" He opened the door. "But I'd better hurry to that examination or I'll get James II mixed up with Henry VIII."

Toward the end of the year, Handel faced his former music teacher. "Herr Zachow," he said as he stood by the organ in the Lutheran church, "I like school and I've learned a lot. Professor Francke has been an inspiration. But I want to concentrate on music."

"How old are you now?"

"Eighteen."

"Mmmm. I would help you. But you're a better musician than I am. Mmmm. Why don't you start composing?"

"I've done some composing. But remember the Calvinists are more conservative than the Lutherans. They still prefer the psalms of David."

Zachow brightened. "I know what you should do. You should go to Hamburg."

"And why Hamburg?"

"Because some of the best musicians in the world live in Hamburg, and because they go in for opera."

"But how would I make a living?"

"You could give music lessons." Zachow thoughtfully drummed the top of the organ with his fingers. "If you like, I'll prepare a letter of introduction. When it becomes known that you've played for the Electress in Berlin, you'll have more pupils than you can teach." He laughed and rubbed his hands together.

Nearly two hundred miles northwest of Halle, Hamburg sprawled in respectable rows on the north side of the river Elbe. Untouched by the horrors of the Thirty Years' War, it was a proud and wealthy city. People were so prosperous that quotations from the stock exchange were distributed during church services. All kinds of art and music were popular and the concert and opera houses were crowded.

By chance, Handel met Johann Mattheson on a hot day in July, 1703. Mattheson, the son of a customs collector, was four years older than Handel. He was well educated, loved music, and had a passion for opera. Soon, he and Handel became inseparable. Johann was personally acquainted with Hamburg's musicians and organs. While viewing the most elaborate organ Handel had ever seen, Mattheson said, "It was built by Arp Schnitger, the greatest organ builder in Germany."

Both Handel and Mattheson wanted to improve their music; and since Mattheson was weak at counterpoint, Handel gave him instructions. Likewise, Mattheson helped Handel become a better melodist.

Soon, Handel had a number of pupils; and among these was the son of John Wyche, the British consul in Hamburg. This distinguished pupil signed up with him as the result of a recommendation by Mattheson.

Although Handel was barely earning enough to pay for his meals and rent, he was supremely happy. His music was improving and he was meeting the most celebrated musicians in Germany. Those musicians, together with the crowded opera houses and concert halls, filled his mind with dazzling dreams for the future. One afternoon, just after he had given the British diplomat's son a lesson on the harpsichord, Mattheson burst into the room.

"How would you like to play for Reinhard Keiser?" demanded Mattheson even before he removed his hat.

Handel stared. "What did you say?"

"I said, how would you like to play for Reinhard Keiser?"

"You mean the one who writes and produces those marvelous operas?"

"Yes, that's the one."

"B-but w-would he want me—an unknown from Halle?"

"Yes, he wants you. He needs a violinist."

Handel's mouth went dry. For a moment he was speechless. Finally, he managed, "I'll do my best."

During the next several days George Frideric tuned his violin and spent every moment practicing. While he practiced, he learned all he could about Keiser. His investigation showed that his new employer was eleven years older than himself, that he was passionately fond of music, that he had devoted himself to music from his early youth, and that he believed opera was the best expression of music.

Most operas were melodramatic: The mortgage would be foreclosed if it were not paid within five minutes. Furious antagonists were about to fight a duel; their pistols were loaded and cocked, but the challenger had forgotten his glasses. When a man was hanged, the rope broke. The poison in the soup was discovered at the last moment.

There was endless violence. Eyes were gouged out. Victims were tortured. There were many stabbings. And often, when the villain's head was chopped off, make-believe blood was caused to flow. The people loved gore and the producers supplied lots of gore.

As Handel played his violin, he studied the audience. Few remained seated while the drama was being enacted. Instead, ticket-holders felt free to walk around, visit, transact business, eat, drink, court, and for excitement, shout insults at the performers. Sometimes they insisted that an aria be repeated.

In these circumstances, Handel could see clearly the effect of each episode, song, or aria. If many people walked out during an aria, it was definitely a failure. But if a patron paused with a chop halfway to his mouth, the aria was a success.

Handel made mental notes of these effects.

Keiser was a brilliant musical composer; but the librettos were written by others; and often the writer merely translated them into German from Italian. Handel absorbed Keiser's techniques. He admired Keiser; but he was horrified by his drunkenness and his frequent use of obscene material in his productions. Soon he began to dream that he might write and direct his own operas; and, if he did, he promised himself they would be as clean as a text from the Bible. Indeed, they might even be on religious subjects.

One day the drama of Handel's life was altered as completely as the scenery between part one and part two of a melodrama. Moreover, it was altered in a most unexpected way. For years Christian Postel had written librettos for Keiser. Then he was converted to Christianity. Postel's conversion stopped him from writing off-color lines.

Keiser was angry. "Don't be a prude!" he stormed. "Double meaning lines are what people like. Without juicy scenes the crowds will stay away. And if crowds stay away I won't be able to pay you." He pounded his desk.

"Nonetheless, I'm now a Christian. I won't write smut." Postel was firm. He would rather starve than to write filth.

But what was the young writer to do? After weeks of prayer, he approached Handel. "I feel the Lord wants me to write a libretto titled the *Passion of St. John*. Would you write the music?"

Handel's eyes danced. "That's the best news I've

had since I've been in Hamburg!'' he exclaimed. ''I'll
start the moment you've finished the libretto.''

''While I'm finishing it, read the Gospel of John,
especially the last chapters. Read them until the
crucifixion scenes come alive in your heart.''

''When will we present it?''

''Next Easter.''

While Handel and Postel were laboring together,
Mattheson left for Holland where he hoped to earn
more money than he had been earning as lead singer
for Keiser. With Mattheson gone and Postel refusing
to write smut, Keiser's popularity skidded. Frequently
he played to half empty halls. Often his box office
receipts were insufficient to pay the singers and
musicians.

After rehearsals for the *Passion of St. John* had been
going on for several weeks, Handel became so excited
he addressed a letter to Mattheson urging him to
return in order to enjoy the opening night.

Mattheson did not return.

The *Passion of St. John* was only a partial success.
Handel was disappointed.

''Don't worry,'' comforted Postel. ''The author of
Ecclesiastes said, 'To every thing there is a season'
(1:1). We haven't wasted our time, for we've learned
a lot about Christian drama.''

Handel soon discovered that Postel was right.
People in Hamburg started to speak about him in a
new and appreciative way. In addition, the number
of his pupils increased. While he was working a new
door opened.

Keiser had been unhappy with Handel for working
with Postel and putting on a rival concert. Now, having a change of heart, he approached him. ''George
Frideric,'' he said, ''I've been writing the music for
a libretto written by Christian Feustking. But I'm

tired. Would you be willing to complete it?''

''Is it filled with off-color lines?''

''No. It's as clean as an empty plate in a shop.''

Handel read the libretto and liked it. As he composed the music he made plans for Mattheson to sing a leading part. This opera, titled *Almira*, was Handel's first success. Day after day the opera house was packed.

Elated, Handel composed music for his second opera. Again he arranged the top singing role for Mattheson. The public didn't like *Nero*. It had to be closed after the third performance.

Mattheson then composed music for *Cleopatria*, another Feustking libretto. *Cleopatria* opened on October 20, 1704. It was a smash hit.

Mattheson starred as the tenor while Handel played the harpsichord. The most breathtaking part was the dramatic death of Mattheson which he performed with great feeling. After this scene, Mattheson exchanged places with Handel at the harpsichord. In doing so, he became the *star* actor, the *star* composer, the *star* singer, and the *star* musician.

At first, Handel merely ground his teeth at this humiliation. With effort he refused to complain. But each day he became more and more reluctant to give up his seat at the harpsichord. After all, he was a much better player than Mattheson.

Finally Handel rebelled.

''Get off the bench!'' commanded Mattheson in a firm whisper.

''I will not,'' replied Handel as he continued to play.

''Off!'' he repeated.

Handel refused to move.

Mattheson glared and tried to pull him off.

Handel glared back and continued to play.

After a long argument during which each began to

shout, Mattheson challenged Handel to a duel. When they stepped into the nearby Goosemarket, the gleeful audience followed. This was the most interesting opera they had ever witnessed!

Handel knew Mattheson was an expert swordsman. Even so he agreed to fight to the death with swords. Not having one, for he had never used a sword in his life, he borrowed one from a friend.

As the pair circled, thrust, parried, the crowd split into rival groups. "Now's your chance, Handel," shouted one side. "Kill him, Mattheson," replied the other side with equal intensity.

While swords clicked and clanged, the musicians circled, thrust, parried, advanced, retreated. Soon, each was puffing from the intensity of the action. Then, as Handel stepped aside to avoid a murderous thrust, he turned his ankle on a cobblestone. For a split second his guard was down.

At that moment, Mattheson aimed at Handel's heart, and lunged forward with every ounce of strength he had. Handel crumpled and stretched out on the ground.

"Bravo!" shouted Mattheson's friends. "You've killed the beast!"

But there was no blood. The point of the sword had struck a large brass button and the blade had snapped in two. Sheepishly, Handel stood up, brushed his clothes and silently returned to his lodgings.

The bitter hatred between the pair remained.

That night, Handel tried desperately to get to sleep. But he could not. The fact that he had tried to kill a man, legal though the action was, haunted him.

Christmas season that year was a cold one. Handel tried to ease his conscience by remembering the candles and trees of the Christmas seasons of his childhood. It was a vain attempt. Next, he focused his eyes on the stars. But instead of comforting, they sneered at him with accusation. He even contemplated Petrina and her kittens. It was wasted effort. Finally, he decided to squeeze the guilt feelings from his system by writing music for a new opera. He faced a sinister wall. His deep wells of creativity were famine-dry.

The constant thought—*You, George Frideric Handel, tried to kill your best friend*—was like a canker in his heart. Utterly depressed, he even had to force himself to eat. Occasionally he wished he had never been born.

Then on December 30, the owner of the opera house persuaded Handel and Mattheson to get together. "If you don't forgive one another, the Lord won't forgive you," he preached. The pair shook hands, embraced, apologized, shared a sumptuous meal, and renewed their friendship. Nonetheless, Handel's feet continued to drag. He was convinced that his hands were permanently soiled in the same manner in which the hands of Lady Macbeth had been soiled.

Early in January, after hours of rolling and tossing, Handel lit a candle and reread the story of the Cross as recorded in John. As he studied the account of the crucifixion, he was again convinced that Jesus Christ had died in his place, that his sins, including his desire to kill Mattheson, had been removed as "far as the east is from the west" and that they would never be remembered. Never! Never! Never!

Deeply satisfied, Handel pinched out the candle and tried to sleep. He could not. His body tingled with a feeling of utter release. He felt like a prisoner who had been condemned to death and then pardoned. He relit the candle, got out blank music sheets, reread the libretto he was working on, and began to compose. Music poured from his pen.

His wells of creativity were as full as ever. Soon the sheets were covered with notes, bars, and rests.

10
Italy

Handel continued to give lessons, compose music for new operas, and play the violin, organ and harpsichord. And each day he became increasingly bored with his work, and with Hamburg. But how was he to escape?

Learning that an organist was needed at Lübeck, both Handel and Mattheson decided to apply for the position. They went by boat accompanied by a farmer. At the Marienkirche they met the authorities who would decide which musician to employ. Generously, Mattheson suggested that Handel play the organ while he demonstrated his skill on the clavicymbal. After each had played, they faced the committee.

"You are both skilled musicians," announced the chairman after a whispered consultation with the other members of the committee. "We like both of you. But, we think it only fair to mention that whoever becomes our organist has an additional obligation." The chairman stared at the floor and nervously twisted the greying horns of his enormous moustache.

"And what's the obligation?" asked Handel, leaning forward.

"He must marry our last organist's daughter."

Both Handel and Mattheson stared. "M-marry the last organist's d-d-d-daughter?" stuttered Handel. His eyes widened into a stare.

"That's our custom. When Dietrich Buxtehude became our organist many years ago, he took to wife the former organist's daughter and now the new organist is required to do the same."

Handel's tongue went dry.

"I know I may have startled you," added the chairman. "But keep in mind that Fräulein Buxtehude is a lovely girl. She's plump, but she's a great cook." He turned to the committee. "Isn't that so?"

"Yes, that's so," agreed one of them. "She can cook sausages until they are absolutely perfect. Next to my wife, she's the best cook in Germany."

Neither Mattheson nor Handel took the job.

In spite of this episode, Handel determined to leave Hamburg. His main reason was that he had learned all that both Mattheson and Keiser could teach him, and he needed some more advanced teachers. He still dreamed of meeting Alessandro Scarlatti. But Scarlatti, and his now equally famous son, lived in Italy. Italy was many weeks away. Not being rich, he realistically wondered how he could make such a trip. He had saved only two hundred ducats, because much money had gone to repay debts to his mother.

Considering the length of the trip, however, two hundred ducats would not last very long. But money, or its lack, meant little to Handel. When he considered pursuing a project, his main concern was: Is this project within the will of God? And after much prayer and Bible reading he became convinced that a trip to Italy was within the will of God. After all, hadn't

God called him to be a composer, and weren't the Italians the best musicians in the world?

When Dorothea Handel read George Frideric's letter announcing that he was leaving for Italy, she was horrified. Facing Anna, she stormed, "Why should he go to Italy where he is unknown when he can remain in Germany where he is known? And how will he get along with the people? They are Catholic; he is Protestant. I'm afraid his father was right. My son will become a vagabond. I can visulize him now sitting on the street in Rome begging for food."

George Frideric, however, had made up his mind; and since his mother could not stop him, she daily lingered at her bedside praying for his success.

The only friend Handel had in Italy was Prince Gaston de' Medici, who lived in a large palace in Florence. But he was most unreliable. Money spilled through his fingers in the manner of dry sand. He chased women, consumed huge quantities of liquor, gambled, and fled from one pleasure to another. His single virtue was that he passionately loved great music. Although he knew he was taking a chance, Handel sent him a letter, informing him that he would be paying him a visit in Florence.

The trip to the Alps and then across them was long. The magnificent snow-covered peaks were inspiring, even though the trip at times was backbreaking. And Handel kept wondering if he was making a fool out of himself. Perhaps he would, indeed, starve.

The coach stopped on the Italian side of the Alps in order to change horses, and Handel went for a walk. Soon he heard organ music. He followed the sound, entered a church, and stood by the side of the organist. When the old man paused, Handel said, "You play very well. And the organ is magnificent."

The old man turned toward him. "And who are you?" he asked.

"Oh, I'm a traveler from Germany. There we have great pipe organs. I once played one built by Arp Schnitger, our best organ builder. Ah, but his organ would not compare to this one."

"Would you like to play something?" The organist motioned toward the keyboard.

"Of course."

After adjusting himself on the seat, Handel touched a few notes and then he played three verses of *A Mighty Fortress*. Adding counterpoint variations and using rich harmony, he made the entire building vibrate with Luther's great hymn. After a mighty conclusion he smiled at the old man. "You have a marvelous organ," he said.

"And who, my friend, are you?" demanded the organist as he wiped his tears.

"Oh, as I told you before, I'm a traveler from Germany."

The old organist accompanied Handel to the door. When he pushed it open, a stream of light illuminated Handel's face. Suddenly a knowing look dominated the old man. Eyes gleaming, he wrapped his arms around his visitor while he exclaimed, "You must be the Celebrated Saxon."

Handel smiled. "I owe you an apology," he said.

"Why?"

"I forgot that I was in a Catholic Church. I should not have played that Lutheran hymn."

"Nonsense! That hymn was inspired by the Holy Spirit. It belongs to all faiths. In time it will be in Catholic hymnals." Handel had just stepped outside when the old man stopped him. "I have a challenge," he said.

"You mean you want to fight a duel?" Handel frowned.

"No, no. My challenge is this: Why don't you write

some great music that will appeal to both Catholics and Protestants?''

"And how would I do that?''

"Write on biblical themes such as Saul, Samson, and perhaps even the Messiah. All Christians love the Bible.''

Handel thanked him and hurried back to the coach.

Handel was welcomed in Florence with enthusiasm by Ferdinand de' Medici, the real owner of the luxurious palace, and elder brother of Gaston. Handel was assigned an apartment that overlooked the city of Florence. With an inspiring view and leisure time, Handel spent several hours each day composing cantatas and rewriting *Almira*. He also wrote a new opera, *Rodrigo*. It was about a king of the Visigoths. He dreamed that he could produce these new operas in Rome. If they succeeded there, all of Italy would be opened to him.

Ferdinand was possessed by one intense passion: Music. He loved it and dipped again and again into his treasures in order to surround himself with the world's finest musicians. He was also intrigued with the possibilities of new musical instruments. With this in mind, he employed Bartolommeo di Francesco Cristofori.

Bartolommeo worked hard, and in 1711 he developed an instrument that was a vast improvement over either the harpsichord or clavichord. He named his new invention *piano e forte*—soft and loud.

Handel's major disappointment at Florence was that Alessandro Scarlatti had moved elsewhere. "Why did he leave?'' inquired Handel of a musician.

"Ferdinand grew tired of the melancholy tone of his compositions. Also, he had been here for three or four years. Ferdinand tires of those he knows too well. He likes change.''

But even though neither Scarlatti nor his son were there, Handel loved Florence. This city on the Arno River in central Italy, bloomed with music, art, museums, history. And, even though the city was a number of miles from the palace where he stayed, he made frequent visits. He loved to walk through its twisting streets. Sometimes he paused at the home of Dante, the famous religious poet whose lines "All hope abandon, ye who enter here," although four hundred years old, were still being memorized and quoted in most major languages. Another place that tugged at his heart was the home of Galileo, the astronomer who discovered a century earlier that Jupiter had satelite moons, and who was nearly burned at the stake because he agreed with Copernicus that the earth moves around the sun.

The vast number of priceless treasures in Florence attracted Handel; and yet many of them pointed to one fact: *Those who make great contributions to the world often have to pay a fearful price.*

The day Handel left for Rome was an exciting one for him. He was a young man, not quite twenty-two, and not only would he see the city where the apostle Paul had laid down his life, but he would also see the Colosseum, and those things which had so deeply moved and changed Martin Luther. His main interest, however, was that he would see his operas, *Almira* and *Rodrigo*, produced. Deep inside, Handel was confident that his operas would be successful.

During his first day in Rome, while riding past the Colosseum, Handel asked, "How many opera houses are there in Rome?"

"None."

"None! And why not?"

"Ten years ago, Pope Innocent XII closed them."

"Why?"

"He said they were cesspools of immorality."

"An opera doesn't have to be filthy."

The coachman shrugged.

Handel was short of money, and now that he could not produce an opera, he wondered how he would pay rent and buy food. A hollow place formed in his stomach. *Was he going to be a penniless beggar as his father predicted?* While he was hanging his clothes in the closet of a room he obtained and hiding his opera scores, there was a sharp knock on the door.

"Yes?" asked Handel. He faced a messenger attired in a crisp blue uniform fringed with gold braid.

"Here's a letter from Cardinal Ottoboni."

"And who's Cardinal Ottoboni?"

"He's the nephew of the Pope." A frown at such ignorance clouded the messenger's face.

The letter read: "As long as you are in Rome, you will stay with me. Please return with my servant. I will pay all of your expenses."

On the way to the Cardinal's palace, Handel learned that Ottoboni was one of Europe's richest men, that his uncle, the Pope, had made him a cardinal when he was only twenty-two, that he loved music, and that he helped the poor with a lavish hand. The coach stopped at the Cardinal's palace.

"I heard about you from your friend Ferdinand in Florence," explained the Cardinal. "His letter declared you are a musical genius."

"Oh, I wouldn't say that," replied Handel. "I just try to follow the will of the Lord."

"And what is your faith?"

"I'm a Lutheran."

"Mmmm. Mmmm. Maybe while you're here you'll receive more light and become a part of the true faith." The Cardinal laughed.

"Your Eminence, I was born a Lutheran and I will die a Lutheran."

"Mmmm. Mmmm. Well, be that as it may, we want to hear you play while you're in Rome. Johann Sebastian Bach is also a Lutheran and some of his compositions are unsurpassed.''

The first time the Cardinal heard Handel play the organ he was utterly spellbound. From that moment on, doors in Rome were flung wide open. Soon, Protestant though he was, he was asked to play the organ at the church of St. John of Lateran, considered by Roman Catholics as the ''mother of churches.''

During this visit in Rome, Handel kept busy. He wrote cantatas, composed music for several of the psalms, learned from famous musicians, visited the same sights that had finally impelled Martin Luther to cry, ''The just shall live by faith!''

A psalm which Handel had put to music was performed in Rome on Easter Sunday. His music fitted the passage as a glove fits a hand and the church authorities were delighted. After that service, Handel's name was on every lip. But Handel was not satisfied. He wanted to meet Scarlatti and his son.

Returning to the north, Handel visited Florence and then headed for Venice, the magic city of islands and boats. He arrived during Carnival Week and found the city of music full of joy. The gondolas were busy. The seven opera houses overflowed. Sidewalk cafes were jammed. Wearing a mask, Handel entered a music hall. There he noticed a man improvising on a clavier.

''Who is that?'' whispered Handel to the man sitting next to him.

''That's Alessandro Scarlatti,'' replied the man.

The moment Scarlatti left his bench, the hall rocked with applause. Handel waited until the clapping had stopped, then he took his place at the instrument. He decided to play a composition of Scarlatti's with his own variations. Scarlatti's music had wide avenues, leaping fountains, waterfalls, the thundering of marching troops. To these, Handel added whirling constellations, salvos of cannon fire, dancing suns, avenues of crimson flowers, the blaze of comets.

After Handel stood, the audience also stood. They shouted, clapped, whistled and demanded an encore.

When there was sufficient quiet, Scarlatti turned to his son, who himself was a skilled player. ''Tell me, Domenico,'' he whispered, ''who is that masked man?''

Domenico shook his head. ''I don't know. But by his playing, I would say that he's either the Celebrated Saxon or the devil.''

After that, Handel revisited Rome and Florence, and wrote and produced several operas. Back at Venice again, he met Ernest Augustus, the younger brother of the Electress Sophia Charlotte and George Ludwig. The two men talked about Germany and Handel told him of the time he played for Sophia Charlotte.

''Why don't you visit us in Hanover?'' Prince Ernest asked.

''When I return to Germany, I just may do that,'' Handel answered.

Prince Edward introduced Handel to the Earl of Manchester, who had just been appointed English Ambassador to Venice. The Earl spoke glowing words about England, and Handel decided he would like to visit there sometime too. Changes seemed about to come to his life.

11
London

Having heard Italy's best musicians, Handel decided it was time to return to Germany. He recrossed the Alps and settled in Hanover, where he had been invited by Prince Ernest. Once there, he learned that Ernest's father had died, and his older brother George Ludwig was now Elector of Hanover, as well as the arch-treasurer of the Holy Roman Empire. He was a powerful and wealthy man.

Just after he was settled, Handel's friend, Agostino Steffani, quarreled with a choir member and resigned his position as *Kapellmeister*.

"And who do you recommend to follow you?" asked the frustrated Elector.

"George Frideric Handel."

Elector Ludwig studied him sharply. "Yes, I've heard about him," he finally said as he smoothed the waist-long hair framing his rather thin face. "My sister, Sophia Charlotte, claims that he's the greatest organist in the world. He played for her in Berlin when he was a child."

Steffani bowed low. "She is right. Nowhere could your Electoral Highness find a more qualified person to manage the musical affairs of Hanover. Handel has magic in his fingers."

"Send him over. We'll consider him."

Handel's appointment as Hanover's Kapellmeister was dated June 16, 1710. It paid a high salary.

Upon being paid the first time, Handel was so startled by the amount of money placed in his hands, he celebrated by going to Hanover's finest restaurant. Seating himself at the best table, he ordered their two most expensive meals. After an hour of impatiently waiting for his order, he summoned the waiter.

"Where are my dinners?" he demanded.

The uniformed man shrugged. "Herr Handel, we know you like your food hot. We were awaiting the arrival of your guest."

"Guest! Who said anything about a guest? I don't have a guest. I'm going to eat both dinners myself."

Handel kept busy. He played the organ, trained

choirs, led orchestras, attended the Lutheran church, and composed music. Hanover with its manicured lawns, tall fountains, beautiful buildings, suited his taste. The political situation was another matter. He kept his ears tuned for every whiff of gossip.

"Elector George Ludwig thinks he may eventually become the king of England," said a choir member with whom Handel was having lunch.

Handel remembered that George was, indeed, descended from English kings. "But he doesn't speak English," objected Handel.

"That doesn't matter. It's the bloodline that counts."

"Is he the heir apparent?"

"In a way, yes; and in a way, no. The heir apparent right now is George's mother, Sophia. But Sophia has the incurable disease of old age." He laughed. "She is now eighty and getting older every day."

Handel cut a piece of sausage. "Why is she the heir apparent?"

"Because she is the *granddaughter* of King James I, while George is the *great-grandson*. She has the advantage of an entire generation."

"But if Sophia became Queen Sophia, would not George follow her to the throne?"

"That he would. However, England's present ruler, Queen Anne, is only forty-five. Still, she has no heirs. All of her seventeen children are dead and she lost her husband two years ago."

"Elector George may then become King George I of England?"

"Correct. But if he does become king he'll have a lot of problems."

"What do you mean?"

"We'd better go outside. Walls have ears and waiters like to gossip."

As the two walked toward Handel's rooms, the choir member patiently waited until they came to a lonely place, then he said, "George Ludwig is a wicked man. He drinks heavily and is immoral. His first wife, Sophia Dorothea, finally got fed up with him. She shook her fist in his face and told him that he'd have to straighten up. But George is stubborn. His wife then decided to teach him a lesson by being as wicked as her husband."

"What did she do?"

"She eloped with Count Philipp von Königsmarck, a good looking colonel of the guards. When George learned about this, he had his marriage with Sophia annulled, and he sent her to prison for life. The colonel disappeared.

"All of this means that his two children by Sophia hate him. The daughter, Sophia Dorothea, hates her father with passion. The son, George Augustus, also hates his father. Now if George Ludwig becomes King George I of England, George Augustus could follow him as George II." The choir member shuddered.

"Will that be a problem?" asked Handel.

"Of course! If George Augustus became king, he'd want to change everything his father did. Herr Handel, I'm frightened."

That night George Frideric thought about the strange careers of kings, and how they could affect his own career. He was growing sick of the tensions in Hanover. England might be a good change. He had bright memories of the enthusiastic descriptions of England related by the Earl of Manchester. From the time he was introduced to the Earl in Venice, he longed to see the place which Shakespeare described as "this scepter'd isle . . . this precious stone set in the silver sea . . . this England."

Mustering up courage, he approached the Elector.

"You have my permission," said George Ludwig. "But return quickly." He pushed away a strand of hair that had crept over one eye. "We need you in Hanover."

Before sailing to England, Handel returned to Halle to visit his mother. From her letters, he knew that she had recently been engulfed with sorrow. His younger sister Johanna Christina had died the year before, and his half sister Dorothea Elizabeth had just lost her first child.

Except for Anna, his mother was living alone.

George Frideric did all he could to cheer his mother. He entertained her, along with Aunt Anna, at the town's best restaurants, accompanied them to church, went with them to the cemetery, placed flowers on his father's grave, and arranged for repairs to be made on the house. He also called on Zachow. He would like to have remained in Halle with his mother. But deep within, he knew that he must go to England.

The leaves on the trees in London which Handel witnessed in the autumn of 1710 were already crimson and brown and were filling the parks. London was a compact city of half a million people. On the north it stretched as far as Russell Square; on the west to Bond Street; on the east to Whitechapel Church; and on the south it edged and leaped the River Thames. London Bridge, the only bridge crossing the river, was crowded with houses. Outlying areas were meadows where cattle grazed and, on occasion, duels were fought.

Sloshing down the streets, sometimes ankle-deep in mud, twenty-five-year-old Handel wondered where he would stay and what he would do. He did not understand English, could not read the signs, knew nothing about the currency, and assumed that he had no friends in the big city. As days and then weeks passed and his loneliness increased, he wondered if he had made a mistake in coming to London. The English kidney pie did not appeal to him. Often he had difficulty consuming just one dinner. Again he remembered how his father had predicted that if he became a musician he would starve.

Heartsick, he thought of the extravagant metropolis the Earl of Manchester had described. That picturesque description was completely opposite to the smelly, disease-ridden city in which he was now living. Frustrated, Handel opened his Bible and prayed. But instead of receiving assurance, it seemed to him that his prayers were being ignored.

During the next several weeks, he again wished that he had never been born.

Sometime in December, Handel noticed a man going from door to door selling coal. Feeling a curious impulse, he approached him.

"Yes?" said the man. "Do you need some coal?"

"No, I no vant coal. I-I-I—"

Suddenly a look of recognition crossed the coal dealer's face. "A-are you George Frideric Handel?" he ventured.

"Dat's vat dey say."

"Well, then you will play for me tonight?" He wrote the address on a slip of paper. "My name is Thomas Britton. Come at seven."

Thoroughly polished and in his best clothes, Handel left his rooms an hour early. To his dismay, the address was in a back alley near Clerkenwell Green. Mud, fragments of coal, broken glass, and other debris littered the area. While he was staring in disbelief, Thomas Britton stepped out of the ground floor of the building. "I store my coal in the back," he explained. "Follow me up the stairs."

Handel could not understand everything he said, but he obediently made his way up the outside steps. As he climbed and sometimes almost crawled, he wondered if he was a victim of a gang of thieves. Every cent he had brought to London was in his pocket. If he were robbed, he would be destitute. He nervously touched his thinning wallet.

At the top of the steps, Handel squeezed through a window. To his immense relief, he noted rows of seats and a harpsichord and several other instruments.

"You are early," said Britton. "Englishmen don't like to come ahead of time. If you like, you can play the harpsichord while we wait." His words were again wasted. But Handel understood that he was to be seated until the audience appeared. Looking about, he shuddered at the smell of stale beer and tobacco. Then he began to laugh. It was outrageous that he, George Frideric Handel, darling of the great churches and music halls of Italy agreed to perform in such a place. Yes, there was no doubt about it. After he used up his savings, he would starve.

While he laughed, two or three well-scrubbed gentlemen squeezed inside. Handel studied them out of the corners of his eyes. Each appeared to be a member of an upper class. And, to his dismay, one of the gentlemen carried a violin, and the other a horn.

Unknown to Handel, the handsome Thomas Britton was a London favorite. It was considered the "in" thing for those who loved fine music to climb the outside steps of his loft which was, according to a writer of the time, "not much higher than a canary pipe, with a window but very little bigger than the bunghole of a cask." Indeed, this door-to-door coal dealer was so famous, London was singing a song about him. The ditty climaxed with the catchy chorus:

Altho' disguis'd with smutty looks,
I'm skilled in many trades.
Come hear me fiddle, read my books,
Or buy my small coal, maids.

Soon the loft was filled, and then crowded. At 7:00 p. m. Thomas Britton stepped to the front. "This evening," he said, "we are highly honored. George Frideric Handel, also known as the Celebrated Saxon, will play for us on the harpsichord."

The tiny ripple of cheers that followed this announcement indicated that Handel was almost an unknown in London. Patiently gritting his teeth, he listened to the other musicians while he awaited his turn. Finally it was his turn to take his place at the small harpsichord. Strangely, he felt just as nervous as he had been when he faced his first audience in Rome. Since many in the room were musicians who loved opera, he played an aria from *Rodrigo*. As he played in the candle-lit room, he was conscious that he was reaching hearts.

The moment he stood to bow, he met with a storm of approval. The audience demanded an encore and refused to stop clapping until he returned to the harpsichord.

From then on for several weeks Handel returned each Thursday and played. He received no money for his work, but he was meeting numerous musicians and this was important. Nonetheless, his wallet was getting dangerously flat.

Early in January, 1711, Handel was startled by a loud knock on his door. "I am Aaron Hill," said the visitor, speaking in broken German. "I've come to see you about two important matters."

"Yah?" replied Handel, pointing him to the only extra chair in his room.

"First, I want to say that you have great talent.

There is no musician in all of England who can compare to you. I would like to hear you play the great organ at Westminster Abbey. If you do, the entire congregation will be breathless.

"But, Herr Handel, there is a great obstacle in your way."

"Yah?"

"You must learn to speak English. Now before I explain to you how easy it would be to learn English, let me tell you something myself. May I?"

"Go ahead."

"When I was a lad I was utterly penniless. Since I had nothing to do but to wander around the streets, I eventually made my way to Constantinople. The British Ambassador there, Lord Paget, was related to me. But when I knocked at his door, I found that he was angry because I had left England. And so there I was, stranded in a strange city with no money. I was desperate.

"What did I do? I learned to speak Turkish. Once I proved that I could learn, Lord Paget had mercy on me and sent me to school. Then he paid my way to Palestine and finally to England. When I got here in 1703 I still didn't have anything to do. But since I had learned Turkish, I had a lot of information about Constantinople and so I wrote *A History of the Ottoman Empire*. That work opened London to me. It made me into a celebrity."

"Do you mean I should write a book?" Handel laughed.

"No, but you must learn English. And English, my friend, is easy to learn. In German you say *Morgen*. In English we say *morning*. In German you say *Tür*. Here we say *door*. In German you say *Schuh*. Here we say *shoe*.

"Many words in German are almost the same in

English. Of course we capitalize differently. I learned when I was studying German that you capitalize nouns, even in the middle of a sentence. We write: Open the *door* with your *shoe*. The Germans write: Open the *Tür* with your *Schuh*. We capitalize *I*, the English word for *ich*, which you write with a small *i*. And we write *you* with a small *y*, while the Germans write *Sie*, their word for *you* with a capital letter."

Handel laughed. "Dat shows ve are better Christians. Ve love our neighbors more den ourselves," he replied in English.

Hill joined in the laughter. Then he said, "Herr Handel, you must learn to say *what* rather than *vat*, and *there* instead of *dere*."

"I'll try. But vat is your udder matter?"

Hill nervously bit his lip. "Opera has been having a hard time in London. Several have failed. You, my friend, can change all that."

"Vat you mean?"

"I have an excellent libretto. It overflows with action and drama. I want you to write the music. It will be your debut. I manage the Haymarket."

"Da Haymarket?" Handel almost fell out of his chair.

"Yes, the Haymarket."

"But dat is da best music hall in London." Handel's mouth went dry.

"Never mind. You, George Frideric Handel, will fill it." He looked deep into his eyes. "Will you write it?"

"I vill. Ven should it be finished?"

"In two weeks."

"Two veeks?" Handel stared.

"Yes, we open on February 24. Here's the libretto."

12
Rinaldo

The moment he closed the door to his room, Handel opened the package containing the new libretto. (It had already been named *Rinaldo*.) The first glance sent chills down his spine.

The dog-eared manuscript was merely a rough outline.

After a sleepless night, Handel faced Hill. "How can I compose music for a libretto in two weeks if da libretto isn't finished?"

"Easy. Rossi will write the libretto, you'll write the music."

"Impossible!"

"It's not impossible. Rossi wrote a play on the subject. Now he merely has to turn it into a libretto."

"Vas da play a success?"

"I don't know."

"And vat about da singers? I need to know dere names so dat I can compose da right parts for dem."

"I've hired the best. Let me see. I have contracts with Boschi and his wife; Nicolini, the best male soprano in Italy; Valentini; Elizabetta Pilotti and Isabella Giradeau.''

Handel stared. When he finally recovered control of his tongue he exclaimed, ''Dey are da best. I know dem all. Now ven vill I see Rossi?''

''He'll be here in a few minutes.''

Since the opera was in Italian and Rossi was Italian, Handel used Italian in his conversations with him. ''Tell me what the story is all about,'' he said.

''It's based on an episode in Torquato Tasso's (1554-1595) epic poem *Jerusalem Delivered*. The action takes place in Jerusalem during the first Crusade. There are two leading persons: the beautiful queen Armida who has supernatural powers and Rinaldo, a leader of the Crusaders. Rinaldo tries not to fall in love with Armida. But finally, he finds her irresistible. Armidà also tries not to fall in love with Rinaldo. She, too, finally succumbs. But then duty calls Rinaldo away. Disappointed, Armida sets her palace on fire, and disappears in the air.''

''Mmmm,'' replied Handel, ''you have enough action for three operas. We only have thirteen days left. Let's get busy.''

As he thought about the singers, Handel wrote parts that would make the best use of each voice. He was especially fond of the voices of Nicolini and Boschi. Boschi was the greatest basso in all of Europe. And Nicolini was a castrato, a male singer whose voice was permanently soprano, made so by an operation in his youth. Inspired, Handel thoughtfully chewed the end of his quill, dipped it into a large pot of ink, and began to compose. Music flowed in a steady stream.

No opera composer believed that a successful aria or march should be discarded. Because of this, Handel spread his old scores on the bed, and proceeded to borrow. With scissors and paste, he used the best sections from *Armida* and others.

Soon Rossi began to complain. "You're writing too fast. I can't keep up."

"Time is passing," countered Handel.

Following ten days of work, Handel was utterly exhausted. Needing a break, he entered his favorite restaurant and ordered coffee. "In four days we'll be finished," he said, addressing the owner.

The fat Italian frowned. "I don't want to discourage you," said the man as he adjusted the apron about his middle, "but you are wasting your time. No opera, especially one in Italian, will succeed in London. Opera is for Italy, not England. But even if you fail, I'll always have a free cup of coffee for you."

"Thanks," replied Handel. "I'll remember that. You serve the best coffee in London."

Rinaldo opened on February 24, the day after Handel's twenty-sixth birthday. From his place at the organ, he could see that every seat was taken. *Ah, but would they cheer or boo?* Handel felt his heart flutter, even when he was improvising on the organ between scenes. He need not have worried. Following a glorious climax, the audience leaped to its feet, cheered, clapped, and shouted: "Author! Author! Author!" When Handel finally got down from the organ, the people roared their approval.

That evening Handel ordered two steak dinners.

But would the Haymarket be filled on the second and third nights? It was. Indeed, in spite of savage attacks in the *Spectator* by the popular writers, Joseph Addison and Sir Richard Steele, crowds continued to surge into the building until it was packed to the doors.

Soon newsboys, milkmen, servants, and members of the upper classes were singing and whistling tunes from *Rinaldo*. The march became a regimental number for the London Life Guards and the aria *Cara Sposa* became a favorite harpsichord number.

In spite of his British fame, however, Handel was not free to remain in England. He was still the Kapellmeister in Hanover, and he felt it was his duty to return. After the London opera season ended, Handel left for Germany. At Düsseldorf, he visited his friends, the Elector and Electress of Palatine of the Rhine, and asked them to write to George Ludwig and his mother, making excuses for his long delay in returning to Germany.

Elector George Ludwig was glad to have his former Kapellmeister back and greeted him with enthusiasm. Soon Handel was busy composing, leading choirs, and giving lessons to George Ludwig's daughter-in-law, wife of George Augustus.

That fall, Handel's older sister gave birth to a daughter. With the Elector's permission, Handel returned to Halle in order to be present at the baby's baptism. While there, he visited his mother and her sister Anna.

"You've no idea how proud I am of your accomplishments," said his mother. "You write great operas, are friends of electors, know kings and queens, and are earning good money. But tell me, son, do you still love the Lord and read your Bible?"

"That I do. I also pray. My faith in Christ means everything."

Again, George Frideric took his mother and aunt to Halle's best eating places, had repairs made to the house, and called on Zachow. Night after night candles in the Handel home burned late. Then he announced that he had to return to Hanover.

Handel kept busy serving as Kapellmeister. But during his spare time he continued a heavy correspondence with friends in London. He also continued to study English.

"Why are you always studying English?" asked a choir member.

"It's a good language."

"True, but you are in Germany where we speak German."

"Learning languages is good for a person," replied Handel. "I already know Latin, French, Italian, and now I'm studying English."

Instead of replying, the choir member merely frowned and walked away.

In the depths of his heart, Handel continued to have a great love for London, even though he still loathed the thoughts of kidney pie and the almost constant presence of ankle-deep mud in the streets. He kept his love for the foggy city until near the end of 1712. Then he approached the Elector.

"Your Electoral Highness," he said, bowing low, "I would like to have your kind permission to return to England."

The Elector studied him a little fiercely. Then, after pushing his long hair away from his face, he asked, "How do you like my second cousin, Queen Anne?"

"I-I really don't know."

"Does she have good health?"

"As far as I know, she does."

"Anne recovered from the disease of smallpox; but she still has the stubbornness of a mule. Don't ever cross her. When she and her sister Mary were girls, they went for a walk in the park. As they were walking along they got into a dispute as to whether an object directly ahead of them was a man or a tree. Mary said, 'It's a man.' Anne replied, 'No, it isn't; it's a tree.' When they got close enough for Anne to see it, nearsighted though she is, it was evident that the object was a man, but Anne said, 'No, sister, it's a tree.' " He laughed.

Handel took advantage of the Elector's good humor and repeated his question.

"Mmmm. Mmmm," mumbled the Elector as he made up his mind. Finally, he said, "Yes, Herr Handel, you may go. But remember you are our Kapellmeister and you must return soon."

When Handel arrived in London he found that opera had slipped out of public favor. The main reason for this, he surmised, was that Nicolini had returned to the Continent and Owen MacSwiney had replaced Aaron Hill as manager of the Haymarket. Mac-Swiney lacked the brilliant dash of Hill and didn't know how to attract crowds. While pondering what to do, Handel learned that Queen Anne would be celebrating her forty-eighth birthday on February 6, 1713.

This was his opportunity.

From a local writer, Handel secured a libretto titled *Birthday Ode*. The text began "The day that gave great Anna birth, who fixed a lasting place on earth . . ." That, he knew, would please her. But, he had never written for a libretto in English, and he still thought in German. What was he to do? The only answer was that he would do his best.

The problem of writing music for an English libretto, however, was a minor one in comparison to the major problem. That major problem was that the right to compose court music belonged to John Eccles. Moreover, a court statute insisted that the chief court musician had to be an Englishman.

Nonetheless, Handel chewed the end of his quill, dipped it in ink, and got busy. He wrote choral passages, solos, duets, and left ample space for himself to improvise on the organ. His main goal was to make the Ode quiver with inspiration. In a few weeks his work was completed. Then, as a result of the fame of *Rinaldo*, he secured permission to put on his concert at St. James Palace.

Alas, Queen Anne was too ill to attend.

Disappointed though he was, Handel put every ounce of effort he possessed into that performance, and the audience loved it. On a later occasion the Queen heard it. As a result of this, and other Handel concerts which she had heard, she rewarded him with an annual pension of two hundred pounds.

Several weeks after Handel was awarded the pension, he was finishing a platter of fish and chips when he overheard some nearby diners discussing his pension.

"It was against the law for Queen Anne to present Handel with such a grant," said one.

"Why?" inquired the other.

"Because the law is clear. I looked it up in my office yesterday. It says: 'No foreigner shall receive a grant from the Crown, or hold office, civil or military.' "

"Then why did she do it?"

His companion laughed. "Because she utterly loathes George Ludwig. By persuading Herr Handel to remain in London, she's taken his favorite musician right out from under his nose. The two hundred pounds are part of her revenge."

Handel only understood part of the conversation. But he was not worried, for he remembered that George Ludwig had said Queen Anne was as stubborn as a mule. That stubborness gave him security.

London was again at Handel's feet. He composed more music, put on concerts, and frequently ordered two meals at a time. He was even summoned to the palace to meet the Queen. On such occasions, the conversation was in French.

Handel had a good income, plenty of food, and time to devour newspaper accounts of world events. He noticed that King Charles XII of Sweden escaped from his imprisonment in Turkey; that Spain ceded

Gibralter to Britain; that Peter the Great, of Russia, married Catherine and went to war against his neighbors; that an infant became the Shogun (Emperor) of Japan.

These distant items provided interesting conversation, but since they didn't affect him directly, he responded to most of them with a yawn, a shrug, or a chuckle. Then in June, 1714, two political earthquakes rocked all of England.

The first event that darkened newspapers was the death of Dowager Sophia, mother of George Ludwig, on June 8. Her death meant that Handel's employer in Hanover was now the heir apparent to the British throne. As he mused on this while finishing his coffee, he wondered what would happen if Elector Ludwig became King George I while he was still in London. Such an event, Handel knew, would place him in an extremely awkward position. It meant that the new king might completely ignore him.

The second June event that jarred England was the passage of the dreaded *Schism Bill*. That legislation decreed that no Dissenter could teach. This discriminating bill, aimed at all who were not members of the Church of England, barely squeaked by the House of Lords with a margin of 5 votes. But it won in the House of Commons by a whacking 111 margin.

The Schism Bill was scheduled to take effect on Sunday, August 1.

A week after the bill was passed, a group of Dissenters called on Handel. "We need your help," said the leader. "And since you are Lutheran, and thus a Dissenter, you can help us."

"How?" replied Handel, frowning.

"You know the Queen. Go to her and explain how really terrible that bill is. It's as bad as some of the decrees of King Henry VIII."

"Please explain."

"Herr Handel, the *Schism Bill* means that no Catholic, Baptist, Lutheran, Independent, or anyone else who does not attend the Church of England, can teach school. And since the Bill becomes law on August 1, all Dissenting teachers will lose their jobs." He shook his head. "It's a terrible law."

Handel shrugged. "I vud like to help, but I'm German."

"True, but Queen Anne likes you. She gave you a pension."

Suddenly Handel had an idea. "Do you men believe in the Providence of God?"

"Of course." All of them, without exception, nodded their heads.

"Didn't you tink dat Queen Anne, a Protestant, came to da throne tru da Providence of God?"

"We did."

"Vell, I'm German, but I knows da story too. Anne vas raised as a Protestant even do her fadder vas a Catholic. Is dat true?"

"That's true."

"When her fadder bacame king, he vas Catholic and his only living son vas Catholic. But da Protestants said dat dis vas not his real son at all, but another baby brought into da room in a varming pan—da kind ve use to varm our feet in Germany when da vinter's cold. Dey accused da king of trying to make England Catholic again, and Parliament trew him out and got a Protestant king. Later, Anne became queen. Yah?"

"You are right." They all nodded their heads.

"God's Providence kept England Protestant. Yah? Now vill not God's Providence help again? Of course it vill." Handel smiled, and signaled for the committee to leave by returning to his work.

During the last part of July, Queen Anne, already

ill, became much worse. Her doctors did everything within their power to save her. They drew pints of blood, used hot irons to raise blisters all over her body, made her continuously vomit, shaved her head and kept her feet smothered in garlic. They were not successful.

Queen Anne died on Sunday morning, August 1, 1714, the precise date the *Schism Act* was to be enforced. She was forty-nine.

A few hours after her death, a college president ordered prayers for His Majesty King George I. "But is Anne really dead?" inquired a student. "She's as dead as Julius Caesar," replied the president.

Church of England bells tolled in the Queen's honor. But many Dissenters found it hard to mourn. Since Anne's death meant that the hated law would probably be canceled and their teachers would not lose their jobs, their churches boomed with hymns of rejoicing.

As Handel awaited the coming of George Ludwig, he was more nervous that he had ever been in his entire life. Would the new king accept him? Would he cancel his pension? Even worse, would he send him to prison for not returning to Hanover after a month or two of absence?

Handel was pacing the floor, thinking of these things, when his eyes noticed a headline in the newspaper. The story was about an infant who had been left on a step with a note tied to her basket. The way children in London were being abandoned by their mothers had long been a concern of his. He reread the news item and then went to a favorite restaurant. But he was so upset he found it difficult to finish the single dinner he ordered.

13
Water Music

At one o'clock, during a warm afternoon on the first of August, George Ludwig was proclaimed King. One of his first announcements was that he would not come to England until Queen Anne's remains were buried.

The Queen's body lay in state in Kensington Palace for more than three weeks, as funeral preparations were completed. On August 23, while a gun on the Tower of London boomed every minute, her casket was moved to the Palace of Westminster. The hearse was drawn by eight horses and covered with purple cloth.

A private ceremony was conducted the next day in Westminster Abbey. The casket was lowered beneath the tomb of Anne's great-great grandmother, Mary Queen of Scots. There, it was positioned amidst the tombs of her ancestors and her beloved husband, Prince George of Denmark.

England hoped that the transfer of power from Anne, who was the last of the House of Stuart, to

George, who was the first of the House of Hanover, would be without incident. But many dreaded, and some passionately hoped that James Edward, the "warming pan" baby, would invade England and be crowned king. Because of this hope—and fear— many slept with leaded guns nearby.

Others had different fears. The Dissenters feared King George would enforce the *Schism Act*. Handel feared he might be sent to the Tower, or to Hanover.

Handel decided to remain quiet and await the outcome. The Dissenters were impatient. A large group of their ministers dressed in black and called on the King.

"Why are you in mourning?" the King inquired.

"Because of the *Schism Act*," replied their leader. "If that Act is enforced, we will have to close our schools, and our teachers will lose their positions."

The Dissenters need not have worried. King George, as was required, attended the Church of England. Nonetheless, he had been raised a Lutheran, and employed Lutheran chaplains. He, himself, was at heart a Dissenteer.

The *Schism Act* was never enforced.

While Handel paced the floor, waiting to learn the details of his fate, he overheard numerous conversations about the new king who couldn't speak English and who didn't have the slightest interest in learning to speak English. Church members were horrified at his morals and the mistresses he imported from Hanover. A boney one was secretly nicknamed the "Maypole," another, "The Elephant." Both were ugly.

The King's many girlfriends inspired a sarcastic nursery rhyme. Boys and girls and even adults enjoyed singing the jingle:

> Georgie Porgie, pudding and pie,
> Kissed the girls and made them cry;
> When the girls came out to play,
> Georgie Porgie ran away.

Hopefuls for high office in the King's court were diappointed when he brought in a large group of former employees from Hanover. These neglected hopefuls came up with another nursery rhyme to express their anger:

> Hark, hark, the dogs do bark,
> The beggars are coming to town;
> Some are in rags, and some are in tags,
> And some are in velvet growns.

That winter, *Rinaldo* was revived; and at one of its many performances, Handel was pleased to see the King and his family in the royal box. This was encouraging, but he still felt that the King considered him an enemy who should be merely tolerated. Then a couple of friends approached him with an idea.

"The King," said one of them, "likes to go out on a barge on the Thames. Why don't you compose some music, rent another barge, move up close to His Majesty's barge and play for him? The King will love it, and it will be easy to raise the money to pay the bills."

Challenged, Handel titled his blank sheets *Water Music*. Hoping to thaw the King's heart, he concentrated every bit of talent he possessed in order to write his finest orchestral composition. From his experience in Hanover he knew the kind of music the King especially enjoyed.

Handel wrote, crossed out, and rewrote. He let his mind leap into the stars, follow the silvery Thames, move with the winds, pause amidst great scenery. He featured trumpts, flutes, horns, oboes, bassoons,

violins and other stringed instruments. Finally the
time came for rehearsal. "Ve must do out best," he
repeated again and again. "If da King likes vat he
hears it will open doors." Renting a barge, employing
fifty musicians, and rehearsing time after time was
expensive. But Handel persisted.

The *Courant* for July 19, 1717 outlined the drama
of that day.

"On Wednesday evening at about eight, the King
took to water at Whitehall in an open barge, wherein

were also the duchess of Newcastle, the Countess of
Godolphin, Madam Kilmaseck, and the Earl of
Okney, and went up the river toward Chelsea. Many
other barges with persons of quality attended, and
so great a number of boats, that the whole river in
a manner was covered; a city company's barge was
employed for the music, wherein were fifty instruments of all sorts, who'd played all the way from
Lambeth . . . the finest symphonies composed express for this occasion by Mr. Handel; which His
Majesty liked so well, he caused it to be played over
three times in going and returning. At eleven, His
Majesty went ashore at Chelsea, where a supper was
prepared, and then there was another very fine concert of music which lasted till two: after which His
Majesty came again into his barge, and returned the
same way, the music continuing to play till he
landed.''

Since the King was obviously pleased, Handel was
encouraged. Still, he wondered if his "exile" was over.
From past experience, he knew that King George was
very temperamental. While he was pondering his fate,
a messenger mounted the barge. "His Majesty would
like to knew who composed that magnificent music,"
he said.

"Tell him it was composed by his servant, George
Frideric Handel," replied Handel.

During the weeks that followed, Handel waited for
a call from the King. There was none. Then he was
stopped on the street. "Geminiani!" he exclaimed.
"What are you doing in London?"

"I lost my job in Naples because no one could
accompany me," said the expert violinist. "I've been
well received in London. But I have a problem. I'm
to put on a concert for the King and I'm worried, for
I will not be at my best unless I can find someone who
can accompany my wild playing; and, as you know,
it's my wildness that people love.''

"You are hard to accompany," agreed Handel. "But I've done it. Remember the time in Vienna?"

"Yes, I remember." Suddenly Geminiani stared at Handel. "Why don't you accompany me?" he asked.

Handel laughed. "I will, if you can get the King's permission."

Since Geminiani could not do his utmost without Handel, he persuaded the King to agree that his former Kapellmeister would be welcome. During the concert, Handel accompanied his Italian friend on the harpsichord and managed to stay with him in spite of his wild swings. The King was impressed. Addressing Handel in German, he said, "I'm confirming the annual two hundred pounds allotted to you by Queen Anne, and I shall instruct the treasurer to keep sending you an additional two hundred pounds."

Handel's cup overflowed. Not only was he let out of exile, but in addition he was promised four hundred pounds a year. The days ahead, he felt would be smooth ones. He would have plenty of time for composition and weekly concerts.

Handel was mistaken.

Toward the end of the year, he noticed that the King was jumpy, nervous. Fearing to inquire the reason, he renewed his habit of studying the newspapers. In them he learned that a sensational news story was breaking. The story centered around the warming pan baby whom many were now calling the Pretender.

Soon after his coronation, King George I dismissed John Erskine—the Earl of Mar—from his job as secretary for Scotland. Humiliated by his dismissal, the Earl decided to raise an army, summon James Edward Stuart from France, conquer England, and have James crowned as King.

At first prople laughed. It seemed impossible that the Earl could have any success. But as the days passed, Londoners were astonished at how the Scots were attracted to him. Soon he had an army of six thousand together with six hundred horses. Also, he was receiving money from France and the Vatican. Moreover, his army was growing. Handel watched these events with a creeping fear. If England became involved in a civil war there would be no place for the type of music he was hoping to write.

More and more Highlanders joined forces with the Earl. The British government decreed death to all traitors. Yet the rebels continued to grow in numbers. Vowing that they would send George back to Hanover and crown James Edward, the Highlanders moved south. Handel held his breath as they took Inverness, Dundee, and Perth.

Even though much of Scotland sympathized with James Edward, the Highlanders refused to cross over into England, and they were finally crushed by King George's army of thirteen thousand. But in spite of the Earl's defeat, James Edward sailed toward Scotland on December 27. He was confident that he would be crowned King.

The Highlanders, however, were unimpressed by James who, at the time of his arrival, was shaking with fever. Also, they realized that their cause was hopeless. Giving up, James fled back to France.

While these events were taking place, music in London was pushed into the background. Handel did a minimum of composing. Then in the middle of June, the King sailed for Hanover and a long vacation. A few days later, Handel also left for the Continent. He was homesick for Halle. And he wanted to see that his mother was financially secure and to spot some musicians he might use later.

14
King Of The Hill

Upon his arrival in Halle, Handel hurried immediately to his mother's home. She was sixty-five. He
found her a little bent but quite happy. Her sister
Anna was still living with her. As before, Handel took
them to restaurants, arranged repairs for the home,
made certain there was plenty of coal for the winter,
and had long visits. Night after night they kept the
candles burning late as they renewed memories and
he related his adventures in London. And as before,
his mother peered deep into his eyes and asked, "How
is your faith in Christ?"

"It's as strong as ever," replied George Frideric.

Handel was saddened to learn that Zachow had
passed away; and, due to a wayward son, his widow
was in need. Generous as always, Handel pressed a
few pounds into her hands. He also assured her that
he would mail additional amounts during the years
ahead. As they parted, he said, "Had it not been for

your husband, I would be nothing.''

In the German town of Ansbach, Handel visited Johann Christoph Schmidt, an old college friend. Learning that Schmidt was having financial problems, Handel had a suggestion. ''You should move to London.''

''London!'' exclaimed the failing wool merchant. ''What would I do in London? I don't even know English. How would I support my family?''

''Arrange for someone here to take care of them, move to London, save some money, and then send for them.''

''Herr Handel, you're dealing with life, not writing an opera. How could I earn a living in London?''

''Simple. You'd work for me.''

Schmidt blinked and his jaw sagged.

''Yes, you can work for me,'' persisted Handel. ''I need someone to make copies of my music, to write letters, to help manage my affairs.'' He laid a hand on his shoulder. ''If you'll return with me, I'll pay your way.''

Working with Handel in London, Schmidt changed his name to Smith. Within a year, he saved enough money to summon his family, including his six-year-old son, to London. English was easy for him. Soon he was speaking it flawlessly and with only a trace of his German accent.

Life was good to Handel. In addition to the four hundred pounds he was receiving from the Crown, he was asked to give music lessons to the Princesses Amelia and Caroline, grand-daughters of King George I. This position kept him close to the Royal Family. It also brought him another two hundred pounds a year. A secure income of six hundred pounds, plus income from operas and concerts provided him with more money than he had ever dreamed of having.

Instead of being a beggar, Handel was rich.

In addition to the income from his profession, Handel invested in the South Sea Company, and the value of his shares was heading toward the stars. A share that sold for one hundred and twenty-eight pounds in the beginning of 1720, brought one thousand pounds that spring.

With riches tumbling in, Handel lived well. He was generous with his tips and charity. Likewise, he ruled London's musical world with a heavy hand. When it was suggested that Londoners were tiring of Italian-type opera, he arched his brows and replied, ''I know vat I'm doing. I vill make da kind of opera I like and da people vill come.'' He strode from triumph to triumph.

During three years of this time, Handel lived in Lord Burlington's palace in Piccadilly. He dined regularly with the greats of the age. And after a concert he made a habit of going to a nearby music hall where he ate rich foods, laughed with musicians, exchanged stories, and ended up by entertaining everyone at the harpsichord.

St. Paul's was a favorite place for Handel. He loved the gigantic organ built by Father Smith and enjoyed giving concerts on it. His recitals always packed the great building to standing room only. And those in charge always begged for his return. For the time being, he was the darling of London.

But gradually empty seats and then rows of empty seats began to appear at his operas. Sometimes the halls were only half full. At first he merely shrugged. He tried more intense drama, sweeter arias, more violins, drums, horns, sensational marches, and better singers. Nothing worked. London was tired of Italian opera.

Face to face with failure Handel wondered what

he would do. Then a miraculous new door opened to him. James Brydges, sneered at by many as the "Rich Rogue," began to beckon.

Brydges had been a Paymaster General. Tens of millions of pounds had passed through his hands and he had become extremely rich. Many suspected that he kept some of the public money. But even though he had been imprisoned in the Tower, the accusation of dishonesty could not be proved. His smile was a wide and permanent one. Indeed, he had been named Earl of Carnarvon and later Duke of Chandos.

Having glittering titles, the Duke built an elaborate palace at Cannons, a theater complete with a huge organ, a magnificent dining room, formal gardens, cottages for servants, art galleries, marble staircases. His servants wore bright uniforms and smartly dressed guards stood at his gates.

Addressing Handel, Brydges said, "I want you to move out to my estate and take care of the music. You

can relax and spend all the time you need composing. Also, you can employ as many musicians as you like and not worry about paying them. If you agree to come, I will instruct the servants to obey your every wish.''

At Cannons, not having to slap out a new opera every two or three weeks, Handel had time to meditate and improve his music. He spent hours at the organ. He took long walks in the formal gardens, let his mind wander as he sat by the fountains, listened to the birds, pondered over his Bible, and considered new types of music. The rhythm of the fountains, the movements of the stars, the flight of birds, the swaying of the flowers suggested a type of music that had not been fully developed—the oratorio.

An oratorio, Handel decided, should be a musical based mostly on biblical scenes; and it should feature orchestras, solos, and choruses.

Handel took many trips to London, was faithful in giving lessons to the princesses, and composed a set of twelve anthems honoring the Duke. But deep inside he longed to stage another opera, and since no major opera had been produced in London during the last two years, he was confident he could write something that would pack the house.

While thoughts of a new opera were churning in his mind, a sensational new idea took form. A group of businessmen decided to launch a Royal Academy of Music. The new company would have access to plenty of money, would hire good musicians, and would be lavish in providing stage props and decorations. Handel was enthusiastic.

Since South Sea stock was soaring, London went mad with stock fever. New stocks were floated daily. Even servants entered the market. Surrounded by this mania, the planners of the Royal Academy of Music financed their venture with five hundred shares of stock.

King George was easily persuaded. He bought five shares for a thousand pounds and promised an additional thousand each year. The King's interest enticed others. Before the ink was dry, the remaining shares were gobbled up by eager buyers.

John Jacob Heidegger, a Swiss who boasted that he was the ugliest man in London, was elected manager. Handel was sent to Germany to employ singers, and Lord Burlington was directed to Italy for the same purpose. A London paper noted: "Mr. Handel, a famous Master of Musick, is gone beyond the sea, by order of His Majesty, to collect a company of singers for the Haymarket."

Handel took advantage of the trip by visiting his mother in Halle. Now sixty-eight, he found her even more bent than she was on his last trip. Also, she was nearly blind. She was in mourning over her daughter Dorothea Sophia. This daughter's death meant that George Frideric was the only one of the children left. He comforted his mother, pressed money into her hand, and did the same for Zachow's widow. Later, on the very day he left his mother, there was a sharp rap at the door.

"Yes?" she asked, straining her dim eyes at the stranger.

"I'm Johann Sebastian Bach," replied the man. "I've come to see that famous son of yours."

"Oh, I'm so sorry. He left this morning."

Bach bit his lip and shook his head. In a tone of deep disappointment, he replied, "I'm indeed sorry that I didn't get to meet him. From what I've heard, he's the greatest organist of our time. I walked twenty-five miles . . ."

Handel was eager to employ the best musicians in

Europe. In Düsseldorf he signed Benedetto Baldassarri and in Dresden he engaged Senesino, by far the most famous *castrato* of that era. He was tall and his soprano voice made people almost breathless. These two, and others, were extremely expensive, but he didn't mind.

From Italy, Lord Burlington returned with Giovanni Bononcini, an eccentric with a magnificent voice. Handel was acquainted with the career of this gentleman, and from the moment he saw him in London he had strong misgivings.

Born in northern Italy, Bononcini had written and produced his first opera when he was only fifteen. By the time he was twenty he was a famous violinist. From then on, he moved from city to city, and in each one played to standing room only. Breaking hearts was his pastime. He became arrogant. While he was in Austria, Emperor Joseph became very fond of him. He showered him with expensive gifts. But when the Emperor needed him for a concert, he refused to appear.

"Do you consider it is an Emperor whom you refuse?" asked Joseph.

"Yes," replied Bononcini. "But you must remember that there are many sovereign princes, while there is only one Bononcini!"

With all this talent available, Handel was anxious to produce his new opera *Radamisto*. He had poured his life's blood into it, and he was certain it would be a success. But he was not in control of the Royal Academy. The directors had other ideas. They insisted that *Numitore* by Giovanni Porta be produced first. *Numitore* opened on April 2, 1720. No one was enthusiastic about it, and it closed five days later. It was then announced that *Radamisto* would open on Wednesday, April 26.

Handel made feverish preparations. Each part had

to be just right. He made minor changes and corrected some of his changes. He rehearsed his musicians. "Ve must do da best ve can," he repeated over and over again. But again he faced disappointment. The directors decided that due to urgent requests by "ladies of quality" a band of French comedians would be featured on the twenty-sixth.

Radimisto was then announced for Thursday, April 27.

As Handel viewed the opening audience, his heart speeded. The King, along with his mistresses, was there; and so was Prince George Augustus. Every seat was taken. The aisles were crowded. There was standing room only. Many were turned away.

Radamisto was an immmediate success. True, it closed after the next performance. But this was due to scheduling. The opera was later revived and was produced in many cities throughout Europe.

Again the man from Germany was king of the hill. How long would it last?

While *Radimisto* was playing, and during the weeks that followed, the owners of South Sea Company stock were getting richer by the hour. Through clever advertising, people of all classes were snared into buying stock. Homes were mortgaged and government bonds sold to raise cash. As the stock soared higher and higher, owners bought coaches, packed restaurants, lived high, wasted money. Instant wealth had made them mad.

Suddenly the stock stumbled and began to fall. Down, down it went. Many thought it would recover. It didn't. It sank like an anchor. A share that brought a thousand pounds in April, brought only three hundred pounds in October, and owners were glad to get one hundred and thirty-five pounds in November. Overnight, coach riders were on foot, or even facing debtor's prison. Some committed suicide. The shiny South Sea Bubble had burst. A bit of doggerel was published in the newspapers:

> Behold a poor dejected wretch,
>   Who kept a South Sea coach of late,
> And now is glad to humbly catch
>   A penny at the prison gate.

Since several directors sold out in time to save their fortunes, bankrupts pointed fingers at them. Blame even focused on King George, for in 1718 he had been elected Governor of the South Sea Company. Others were more severe: "The King is German, isn't he? The problem is with the Germans."

This kind of wrath, as illogical as it was, was turned on Handel for, as everyone knew, he was German and had worked for the King in Germany.

Handel's loss on his South Sea stock was a minor blow. What really staggered him was his loss of popularity. And that humiliation was worsened by the fact that Lord Burlington persuaded the Academy directors to ask Bononcini to lead a rival opera. This meant that patrons had a choice of being entertained by either Handel or Bononcini.

Soon the "war" between the rivals acquired political dimensions. Handel was favored by the Whigs. Bononcini was favored by the Tories and those who had lost money in the South Sea Bubble. The fierce struggle between the two was spread before the public in a jingle written by John Byrom.

> Some say, compar'd to Bononcini,
> The Mynheer Handel's but a Ninny;
> Others aver that he to Handel
> Is scarcely fit to hold a Candle.
> Strange all this difference should be
> 'Twixt Tweedle-dum and Tweedle-dee!

15
Thunder

The Duke of Marlborough died on June 16, 1722. Since all agreed that the victor of the Battle of Blenheim deserved the best, elaborate funeral services were planned. Burial would be in Westminster Abbey.

Who would write the music? Most were certain the assignment would go to Handel. They were mistaken. The honors went to Bononcini. This was like ground glass in Handel's eyes. But he did not retreat. After a few painful hours, he said, "I vill now write da best opera dat has ever been produced in London."

Where would he get his libretto? After refusing several, he selected one written by an old Italian friend Nicolo Francesco Haym, author of *Radamisto*. It was titled *Ottone*. As he composed, it seemed imperative that he get the best soprano in the world.

"I know just the one you need," announced his harpsichordist, Pietro Giuseppe Sandoni. He spoke with utmost confidence.

"Can she sing?"

"Like a nightingale."

"How about her range?"

"It's the widest in the world." Sandoni shook his head, closed his eyes and made a V with his arms. "Herr Handel, she can touch the stars. You'll be breathless."

"Is she expensive?"

"Of course! She's the darling of Naples and Vienna. But she'll make—" He smacked his lips. "She'll make your opera the best London has ever had. There will be standing room only."

"Could we get her for a thousand a year?"

Sandoni clasped his hands as if he were going to weep. "I'm afraid not. But, perhaps, if you double the amount—"

"Excellent. Go to Italy and bring her back. Tell her we'll pay two thousand pounds a year. Now I'd better prepare an aria worthy of her." He started to write. Then, just as Sandoni opened the door, he raised his hand. "What's her name?"

"Francesca Cuzzoni."

Inspired by her possibilities, Handel wrote an aria with wide swings and almost impossible high notes. *Ottone*, he decided, was the ideal opera to open the season on October 27. Alas, the twenty-sixth came and there was no word from Cuzzoni. An old opera had to be used to fill the time.

In the middle of December, Sandoni knocked on Handel's door. "I've brought the singer," he announced. He pointed to a short twenty-three-year-old. "But her name is not Cuzzoni."

Handel stared. "Then, who is she?"

"She is the *former* Francesca Cuzzoni. She is now Signora Sandoni."

Handel's eyebrows arched. "Y-you m-mean y-you m-m-m-married her?" he demanded.

"Yes, Herr Handel, I married her."

As Handel viewed the star of his new opera he had strong misgivings. She was ugly, poorly dressed, squat, ridiculous in manner; and, from his observation, not a good actress. Drama was utterly foreign to her. That he could make her into a prima donna who could capture the hearts of audiences seemed an impossibility.

At that moment he was certain that he had wasted two thousand pounds and that his new opera wouldn't last a single night. He could already see the audience standing and hear their boos.

Handel's first clash with Cuzzoni erupted during the initial rehearsal. "This is the way this aria is to be sung," he said.

"But I don't like it that way," replied Cuzzoni.

"I'm the director. You will sing it my way."

"I will not."

Handel glared, he seized her by the waist and pushed her toward the window. In French, he said, "Madam, you are a female devil. But I am Beelzebub, the chief of devils. Now this is the way I want you to sing your aria." He gave her a demonstration.

Cuzzoni sang it, but in a drastically different way.

Quickly Handel lifted her from the floor. "You will sing it my way," he said, his voice as firm as that of a sergeant in the army, "or I will throw you out the window."

She sang it his way and Handel was extremely pleased. She had a glorious voice.

Ottone opened on January 12, 1723. Handel faced an opera house overflowing with London's best dressed music lovers. Furs, hoops, swords, opera glasses were everywhere. As the curtain went up, Handel had one prayer: *Lord, help Cuzzoni and the other singers to do their best.*

Soon Cuzzoni was on stage. As she held onto unbelievably high notes, trilled, swept the stars and plunged into the depths, the audience leaned forward and held its breath. At the peak of her aria, a man in the gallery was unable to control himself. "She has a nest of nightingales in her belly." he shouted.

The applause at the close was the greatest Handel had ever heard.

On January 15, a newspaper stated, "Today . . . there is such a run . . . tickets are already going at 2 and 3 guineas. . . . It is like another South Sea Bubble."

Ottone ran to full houses for eleven nights. Some tickets sold for over five pounds, a spectacular price.

During the fourth opera season, the Royal Academy presented Bononcini's *Farnace* on November 27, 1723. Since the audience didn't like it, *Ottone* was revived, much to the delight of everyone. By this time the London public was almost unanimous in believing that Handel was the victor in his battle with Bononcini. Some of his proud followers even said:

> Next to Mynheer Handel
> Bononcini can't hold a Candle.

Encouraged by success, Handel bought a four-story brick house in Lower Brook Street near Hanover Square on the West Side of London and hired servants.

But the Royal Academy was not well. People were tiring of opera again, especially Italian opera, and box office receipts were frequently insufficient to pay the bills. Once, instead of paying dividends, the directors requested each stockholder pay an assessment of five percent. That assessment hurt the stockholders decreased attendance.

Desperate to save the company, the directors came up with a unique solution. They decided to hire another soprano to rival Cuzzoni. By balancing one against the other, they could lower the salary they paid each of them. With this in mind, Faustina Bordoni was employed. The *London Journal* brazenly announced: ". . . a famous Italian Lady is coming over to rival Signiora Cuzzoni."

Handel was furious. But since he was not a director he could only stand by and watch. He knew that two rival sopranos in the same house meant disaster.

Faustina was as beautiful as Cuzzoni was ugly. Within months each despised the other, and each had attracted followers. These followers upset the performances by booing the other side. This confusion kept getting worse until it exploded in a terrible scene while Bononcini's opera *Astianatte* was being played in early 1727.

Upset by the booing and catcalls, the prima donnas lunged at each other. They screamed, slapped, scratched, pulled hair. Then the audience rushed to the stage and each faction attacked the other. Seeking objects with which to strike their enemies, they tore up the scenery.

Within hours, pamphlets about the "fighting cats" were being readied for the presses. Former friends became enemies. The Duke of Bedford went to France and fought a duel with the Duc d'Orleans in order to prove that Faustina was an angel and Cuzzoni a devil.

While these quarrels were tearing musical London apart, Handel tried to take his mind off his troubles by becoming a British subject. He took his oath of allegiance in the House of Lords on February 14, and six days later the King signed the bill that confirmed his change of nationality.

King George died on June 11. Prince George Augustus was then immediately proclaimed King George II. This change of monarchs worried Handel, for his close ties with George I annoyed George Augustus who still bitterly loathed his father for imprisoning his mother.

Would King George II cancel his pensions? Caught in a corner, Handel could do nothing but wait. But he did not have to wait long. An imperial messenger brought him a letter which requested him to compose the coronation music. Handel read the letter, smiled, and got busy.

His pensions were secure.

While he considered the portions of Scripture to use in the music, a top ecclesiastic informed him that he would select the needed passages. Handel bristled. "I know my Bible vell. I vill select da proper passages myself," he replied. He chose I Kings 1:38-40; Psalm 21:1; Psalm 89:14-15; and Psalm 45:1. Each selection emphasized the King's need of the Lord.

Handel and others continued to write opera, and the Royal Academy continued to produce them. But the Company was sick. The singers frequently had to sing to near-empty houses. In this condition, the directors decided to revive a patriotic number by Handel. *Riccardo Prime, Rè d'Inghilrerra*, with libretto by Paolo Rolli was well done, and they had great hopes that it would appeal to audiences. And, to insure its success, they used their best singers: Cuzzoni, Faustina, Boschi, Baldassarri, and Senesino, the sensational castrato.

The public did not respond well, and the opera was forced to close after eleven performances. Then, making matters even worse, on December 23, 1727, the directors demanded that each shareholder pay an additional five percent to at least keep the Company limping along.

The final blow to the Royal Academy came from a totally unexpected force. On January 29, *The Beggar's Opera* began to play in the Lincoln's-Inn Field Theater. This opera, written by John Christopher Pepusch, for a libretto written by John Gay, was completely different from anything Handel had ever written. The hero of the story was Captain Macheath, a highwayman who was in love with Polly Peachum. Macheath was imprisoned, but was finally pardoned on the day set for his execution.

This plot was laced with political satire and old English and French melodies. Pepusch even helped himself to Handel's famous march in *Rinaldo*. Some of the dialogue was off-color; and since it made a hero of a criminal, it was denounced by church authorities. But audiences loved it.

The Beggar's Opera packed the theater for ninety days, a much longer run by far than Handel had ever achieved. Its tunes were whistled and sung everywhere. With sinister glee, Henry Carey captivated the crowds by singing:

> She has fired the town, has quite cut down
>   The opera of Rolli;
> Go where you will, the subject still
>   Is pretty, pretty Polly.

Now desperate, the Royal Academy tried several other operas. None succeeded. After eight years of operation, the Company was forced to close. A notice in the *Daily Courant* for May 31, 1728, read:

> The General Court of the Royal Academy of Musick stands adjourn'd till 11 a-Clock on Wednesday the 5th of June next, in order to consider of proper Measures for recovering the Debts due to the Performers, Tradesmen, and others; and also to determine how the Scenes, Cloths, etc. are to be disposed of, if the Operas cannot be continued. . . .

Convinced that Italian opera had no future in London, Senesino, Cuzzoni, Faustina, Boschi and other singers fled to Italy. On the surface, it seemed to those who knew the facts that Herr Handel and those like him were finished.

But neither Handel nor Heidegger was ready to surrender. In their minds, they had merely lost a battle, not the war. Across a table they made bold plans for the future. They decided to launch a company which they alone would direct. They named their fresh venture the *New Royal Academy*.

Since Handel was willing to risk his savings of ten thousand pounds, Heidegger put up an equal amount. In addition, convinced of the soundness of their scheme, King George II agreed to provide an additional one thousand pounds each year.

Handel's next problem was to secure singers, so he headed for Italy.

16
Storms

Since he had twenty thousand pounds, Handel's blood tingled. He thought he could secure the best singers in Italy, but he was mistaken. Reports of the Royal Academy's failure had spread.

Cuzzoni was not interested, nor was the recently married Faustina. Both Handel and Heidegger agreed that Farinelli was a must. Handel approached him. Farinelli listened politely but shook his head.

"We'll have the best opera London ever had," coaxed Handel.

Farinelli shook his head again.

"I'll write special parts for you."

"I'm sorry." Farinelli stood up, ending the interview.

Handel did not give up. He arranged an interview with Anna Strada. Facing her, he almost shuddered, for she was even uglier than Cuzzoni. But he was overwhelmed by her voice. Better yet, she accepted a contract, and so did several others.

Amidst this hiring campaign, Handel received a

letter informing him that his mother was seriously ill.
He returned immediately to the city of his boyhood.
He found that his mother was totally blind, had suffered a stroke, and could only move from one room
to another by painfully shuffling across the floor with
a crutch. As he peered into her withered face, he knew
that he would never see her again. While he tried to
make her comfortable, there was a knock at the door.

"I'm Wilhelm, the eldest son of Johann Sebastian
Bach," announced the caller. "Father sent me to tell
you that he would like for you to visit him in Leipzig. He's not been well."

"I would love to visit him," replied Handel. "But
as you can see, Mother is quite feeble. I must spend
every minute I can spare with her. Extend my
greetings to your father. To me, Johann Sebastian
Bach is the greatest organist and composer of organ
music in Europe."

Handel's eyes filled with tears when he left his
mother. But he had obligations in London. According
to plans, he had to select a libretto, write the music,
and open a new opera by December 2, 1729.

The singers drained much of the Company's
money, and he hadn't an adequate person to take the
male parts. What was he to do? Margherita Merighi
had a deep alto voice. She would have to do the male
parts.

With his candles burning late and his eyes on the
calendar, Handel wrote a new opera in two weeks.
People didn't like the opera, but they liked the lead
singer, Anna Strada.

Lotario was a failure.

The next opera and its two followers also failed to
pay their way. Alarmed, Handel and Heidegger went
into conference. The solution, they decided, was to
hire better singers, even though they cost more money.

Working through the English envoy in Florence, they were able to rehire Senesino; and, through other contacts, they secured Giovanni Commano, an excellent basso.

Handel was encouraged. With an excellent libretto titled *Poro* at hand, he concentrated on making it into something London would love. In the midst of his work, he learned that his mother had passed away. She lacked only a few weeks of being eighty.

To the one who arranged the funeral, Handel sent a letter of thanks:

> I am unable even now to hold back the flow of my tears. But the All Highest has been pleased to enable me to accept His holy will with Christian fortitude. Your thoughtfulness I shall never forget until, after this present life is over, we are reunited, which may the All Good grant us in His mercy. . . .

Forcing himself to keep working on *Poro*, he finally finished it. The curtains lifted on this new opera in February, 1731. Filled with stirring new music, *Poro* was a moderate success. It played for sixteen nights and more than paid its way.

During the rest of that year, Handel did not compose a line. He was grieving over his mother.

Ezio, the first opera produced in 1732 was a failure. Other operas were written and produced. None was successful.

While Handel paced the floor, trying to think of a way to keep the New Royal Academy going, he faced a perplexing problem. The year before, John Rich, producer of *The Beggar's Opera*, brazenly announced that "because of the desire of several persons of quality, he would produce *Acis and Galatea* composed by Mr. Handel."

Handel was shocked. This was done without either

his knowledge or consent. But since copyright laws were not firm, he was quite helpless. All he could do was to grind his teeth and be patient. Perhaps it would not happen again. It did happen again.

In 1732 Bernard Gates decided to do the same thing with another of Handel's works, music composed at Cannons titled *Haman and Mordecai*. Gates added text and without wincing opened *Esther, an Oratorio* on February 23, Handel's forty-seventh birthday.

Again, Handel ground his teeth. *Esther* was *his* work, every note of it. But under the law he could do nothing.

The public loved *Esther* which was, undoubtedly, the first oratorio ever produced in England.

Although Handel was unable to stop the use of his music by others, he found a way to make use of this oratorio himself. Readers of the *Daily Journal* on April 19 were confronted with an advertisement:

> By His Majesty's *Command*. At the King's Theater in Haymarket, on . . . the 2nd . . . of May will be performed, *The Sacred Story of Esther: an Oratorio in English*. Formerly composed by Mr. Handel, and now revised by him with several Additions. . . . There will be on the stage. . . . The musick is to be . . . (in) the manner of the Coronation.

Desperately hoping that this type of entertainment would improve his fortunes, Handel increased the size of his orchestra with additional flutes, violins, oboes. He could not afford the extra musicians, but was convinced that this was the only way to avoid bankruptcy.

Money for *Esther* was not his only problem. Another was to get his Italian singers to sing English without accent. This being impossible, he hoped their added vowels might brighten the work. In his mind's eye, he could already see smiles on the faces of his audience. as Anna Strada added an *a* to all the English words ending in consonants.

London enjoyed *Esther*. And on the night the King and Queen attended, many were turned away. The oratorio had to be repeated five times.

Esther's success made Handel's forced smile real, and it increased his appetite. Alas, he soon found an abyss dark with new problems.

Whenever it was announced that King George and Queen Caroline were going to attend an opera or oratorio, the attendance increased dramatically. Then King George decided to vacation in Hanover. Indeed, he took up with a new mistress and stayed there for two years. Queen Caroline remained in England; but without the King to escort her, she seldom attended public gatherings. The resulting empty box at Handel's musicals, severely reduced the attendance.

Londoners wanted to be seen with their King.

An even worse blow to Handel stemmed from the royal family itself. In this royal family, the generations always seemed to hate each other. So, true to form, the King and Queen hated Prince Frederick.

Once upon seeing Frederick crossing the courtyard, Queen Caroline turned scarlet and shouted, "Look, there he goes! that wretch! the villain! I wish the ground would open at this moment and sink the monster to the lowest hole in Hell!" Frederick, in turn, was angry because his father wouldn't allow him to have an official residence, and because he limited him to an income of 38,000 pounds a year, even though a laborer was fortunate to earn two pounds a month.

Retaliating against his parents, Frederick gathered a pack of aristocratic hoodlums, and went around London smashing windows and making a nuisance of himself. Eventually he thought of a more sinister way to get even with his parents. Since both of them adored Handel, he would start an opera company and ruin him.

Licking his lips with fiendish anticipation, Frederick launched a new company called *Opera of the Nobility*. Since money was no problem with the Prince, he spent freely. He leased the theater in Lincoln's-Inn Fields, and lured many of Handel's most glittering singers, including Senesino, into his fold. He even persuaded Cuzzoni to return to London.

While the Prince used theater to ruin Handel, others used the pen. Attacking Handel was a riskless way to attack the King without being sent to the Tower. On April 7, 1733, the *Craftsman* published a blistering attack. Handel's eyes burned as he read:

> The rapid rise and progress of Mr. H----l's power and Fortune are too well known . . . to relate. Let it suffice to say that he has grown insolent . . . that he thought nothing ought to oppose his extravagant will. . . . No instruments were admitted, but such as flattered his ears, though they shocked those of the audience. Wretched scrapers were put above the best hands in the Orchestra. No Musick but *his own* was . . . allowed, though everybody was weary of it. . . .

The author hid his identity behind this diatribe by signing his name P--lo R--li.

Another attack that cut deeply was a hateful cartoon. It was drawn by Joseph Goupy, the Prince's drawing teacher and the one who had designed scenery for many of Handel's operas. The grotesque drawing showed Handel sitting before an organ. His face was made to resemble the snout of a pig and the floor was strewn with oyster shells, which were to ridicule Handel's appetite for gourmet food.

As the storms rocked his career, Handel's fortunes sank lower and lower.

In the midst of his discouragement, Handel received a startling invitation to put on a series of musicals at Oxford University some fifty miles northwest of London. The occasion was that of conferring degrees, both earned and honorary. Handel was flattered. But since the Prince had raided his top musicians, he wondered how he would replace them. Senesino shook his head. "I'm not interested," he replied.

Fortunately, Anna Strada remained loyal, as did several others. Still there was a shortage. Eventually, he summoned his cook to sing bass.

Handel and his hundred musicians dismounted from their carriages in Oxford on July 4, 1733. He was amazed at the stir he caused. The university town was so crowded many were forced to sleep in the streets. He put on two concerts a day and each time there was standing room only. Even his rehearsals were jammed.

A student approached Handel one day and said, "Sir, I want to tell you that your oratorio about Esther stirred me greatly. It made me want to be a better man."

While he was enjoying this unexpected popularity, a gowned official from the university faced him. Said the man, "Herr Handel, we've decided to give you an honorary degree."

"An honorary degree?" Handel's jaw sagged.

"Yes, you are the greatest musician in England and we will be honored if you accept it."

Handel stared. "And vat are de requirements?"

The man shrugged. "Well, we would like a little donation of five hundred pounds."

"Five hundred pounds!" exclaimed Handel, his eyes shooting fire. "No, I don't vant. But tanks yust da same."

After the official had gone, Handel turned to a friend and remarked, "Vy should I trow my money avay for vat de blockheads give me? I vant not such honors."

Handel loved honors. And he could have afforded the five hundred pounds. But his recent troubles and the atmosphere at the university seemed to be working a change in him. Charles Wesley had graduated from Oxford just a few months before and his influence had left students fired with spiritual purpose to follow the Bible. Seeds for Handel's own spiritual renewal were being planted, and buying a degree did not fit in.

Handel left Oxford with a new and determined glow in his eyes. Back in London he found that he was still under attack. People pointed and jeered when he stepped out of his carriage. They ignored his operas and concerts. Money ran short. He could not pay his bills. When debtor's prison threatened, Heidegger had a suggestion. "All we need to do is put on something like the *Beggar's Opera*—"

"And use double-meaning vords?" interrupted Handel.

"And why not?"

"I vill not do it." He got up and paced around. "God gave me a talent. He vants me to use it as a vitness to His love and dat is vat I vill do. My trust is in God."

"And go broke?" Heidegger made a face.

"Yah, and go broke. I vill not use vicked vords. Dey can burn me at da stake before I vill use dem."

Handel and Heidegger dissolved partnership. A newspaper summed up the situation by declaring that the closing of their company was a "triumph for the debtors of a brace of madmen."

17
Paralyzed!

With no ready cash, and having been forsaken by most of his best singers with the exception of Anna Strada, George Frideric Handel appeared to be finished. Even formerly close friends considered him a has-been and openly snubbed him. But deep within his heart burned a tiny, ever so tiny, candle of hope.

As he considered his place in the corner, a vicious new stream of ridicule, aimed at him, began to spice the London papers. The gleeful verdict of numerous writers was that the overweight German was already a dim memory. On one extremely depressing morning, he faced a stack of overdue bills and discovered a new poem about himself in the latest London paper. Although the lines were edged with hate, they were clever.

> The Figure's odd—yet who would think?
> Within this Tunn (of meat & Drink)
> There dwells the Soul of soft Desires,
> And all that Harmony inspires:
>
> Can Contrast such as this be found

Upon the Globe's extensive Round;
There can—yon Hogshead is his Seat
His sole Devotion is—to Eat.

Handel reread the poem, slumped into his chair and remained there for a long, terrible moment. The cruelty of the lines cut into his heart. Then he forced himself onto his feet, powdered his wig, and strode briskly into the street. He approached each creditor, signed a note for his overdue bill, and solemnly assured each one, "I vill pay you later."

His candle still flickering, Handel was convinced that he could soon write something that would pull him out of the financial pit into which he was being pressed. But while he was considering various librettos, he was struck by another staggering blow. Prince Frederick outmaneuvered him and obtained the new lease on the King's Theater in the Haymarket.

Handel had to settle for the now decaying theater in Lincoln's-Inn Fields. He waded through mud and sidestepped a pair of drunks as he surveyed the district. It was far worse than he had imagined. And the idea that he had to work in such a place was discouraging. But he was broke and thus had no alternative. Gritting his teeth, he produced *Ariadne*, an opera that had previously been successful. This time it wasn't.

Desperate because of the money lost on *Ariadne*, Handel bent his conscience and put on *Il Pastor Fido* and featured a slightly risque French dancer. This production pushed him deeper into debt.

While Handel was staring at empty seats, the Opera of the Nobility was playing to standing room only. The Prince's money had secured Cuzzoni and the male soprano Farinelli, who had become the sensation of London. Concerning, him, a critic wrote: "What a Pipe! What modulation! What ecstacy to the Ear!"

It was a must in London to hear Farinelli, and the people showered him with gifts. The Prince presented him with a gold snuffbox ornamented with diamonds. Taking advantage of his popularity, Farinelli demanded, and received five thousand pounds a year. This was more than double what Handel paid his top singers.

Handel's ship was sinking and as waves lapped over the side, people jeered. What was he to do? As the Christmas season of 1734 approached, John Rich, producer of *The Beggar's Opera*, faced him with a proposition.

"Herr Handel," said Rich, "I have just finished my theater in Covent Garden. I would be proud to have you as my first tenant."

"I'm out of money."

"Nonsense! You'll never earn money working in the slums. Beggars don't like musicals. Move to Covent Garden. Your credit is good."

The crowds increased at Covent Garden and night after night rows of glittering carriages parked before his theater. Handel at last had hope that his debts would be paid. But he was gradually confronted by another problem: illness and depression. Sometimes he lost his will to live, and his joints and right arm often pained him until he was in agony when he played the organ. Soon he was limping on a cane. Night after night his aches were so severe he was unable to sleep. But in spite of his agonies, he continued to dip his quill and write more and more operas.

While straining every fiber to retain his musicians, compose better music, and pay his creditors, Handel created the musical score for his best recent work, *Alexander's Feast*. This brilliant oratorio packed the house. One night alone the box office receipts were four hundred and fifty pounds. If this prosperity continued, he would become debt free.

But this prosperity did not continue. Within days he was upset by trouble that erupted from the palace.

King George II arranged a marriage for Prince Frederick. Handel was ordered to write the wedding music, and this he did, for he still held the position as court composer.

The Prince made it a point not to thank him for the music. The snub hurt. But within a day or two Handel decided on a daring move. He decided to ignore the snub, overlook the devious ways the Prince had tried to destroy him, and compose a magnificent cantata that would honor the heir to the throne. In doing this, he was offering the right cheek to the one who had smitten him on the left cheek.

Two weeks after the wedding, before a house filled with royalty, dukes, earls, lords, and high officials of the court, Handel presented *Atalanta*. His music was filled with love, tenderness, passion, adoration, fulfillment. The guests were delighted, and so were the

Prince and Princess. Indeed Frederick was so over-whelmed that he made friends with Handel, closed the Opera of the Nobility, and started attending concerts at Covent Garden. George Frideric Handel's victory was clear. By using a Christian principle, he turned an enemy into a friend.

Basking in his victory, Handel enjoyed the first peace he had experienced in months. His victory, however, turned out to be a false one.

"I will not be seen in the same place with the Prince, even though he is my eldest son," said the King. He then canceled the one thousand pounds a year he had been paying to subsidize Handel, and left for Hanover in order to be comforted by his German mistress.

Handel was so dazed by this reaction that he went into seclusion.

Missing the portly figure of the opera writer in his favorite restaurants, reporters wrote that he was dying. The truth was that he was having mental troubles. His horrified servants watched him pace around in a trance, talk to himself, address imaginary audiences, kneel before imaginary kings. Frequently he got sunsets mixed up with sunrises. And while he lived in an imaginary world, he often cried out in acute agony, "Oh, my arms, my legs."

In his rational moments Handel discovered the only way to protect himself from horrifying visions and pain was to work. He always felt better when he was composing. Feverishly he began *Giustino* and finished it in a month. Then he completed *Arminio* in twenty-two days.

Both operas failed.

On a damp morning, while fog crept into every corner, Handel awakened to find that his right arm was paralyzed. He could neither move his fingers nor his arm. He hobbled over to the organ and tried to play a single melody. He could not. His right arm refused to move toward the keyboard. Staring into space, he wept.

Handel decided to vacation at Aix-la-Chapelle. Perhaps the hot mineral water would help. With the use of his cane, he made his way to the depot and mounted a carriage headed toward the nearest port.

Handel was hopeful that the sulpher-smelling baths in this northern capital of Charlemagne would be helpful, for he had previously used the mineral baths at Cheltenham Wells in southern England and they had invigorated him.

The bumpy coach trip on the Continent to western Germany took many days. Handel was obliged to make numerous route changes, sleep in filthy, poorly-heated inns, subsist on tasteless food. But when at last he arrived and stretched out for the first time in a steaming bath, he knew it was worth the effort.

Luxurious hot mineral water pushed up from the bowels of the earth and filled wooden tubs. Here the depressed man immersed himself.

But during the first week, in spite of the warm caresses of the mineral water, Handel's mind lingered on his troubles. He thought about his indebtedness, the singers who forsook him, the new animosity of King George II, his paralyzed right arm, the crowds that stayed away from his operas. The memory of each problem plunged his spirits into deeper and then deeper gloom. In agony he asked himself: Is life really worth living?

By the second week, however, Handel began to feel better; and, as his health improved, so did his outlook on life. Late one afternoon while he was soaking, he decided to make a game of counting his blessings and the way he had been helped by God's Providence. While his past moved before him like an action-filled opera, his spirits crept higher and higher.

Soon he was almost chuckling as his mind leap-frogged back to the time he took off by foot and caught up with his father's coach. The fact that the wheel of the carriage twisted off at just the right time enabled him to catch up with the coach. Had it not been for this *accident* at the *right* time and at the *right* place, he would not have accompanied his father to Weissenfels. And if he had not accompanied him, the Duke would not have ordered his father to give him music lessons.

Then his mind moved forward to the time he had fought a duel with Johann Mattheson. He still felt a sense of guilt when he remembered the hatred that dominated him when he tried to kill his old friend. On that occasion, had it not been for the large button on his jacket, Matteson's sword would have killed him. How had he escaped death? By God's Providence.

Other incidents in which the Lord helped also came to his mind. He especially remembered when he was being ignored by King George I. It was during this time that he was stopped on the street by his old friend Geminiani. Geminiani arranged for him to accompany him as he played his violin before the King. And because of that he was restored to royal favor.

Yes, God had been guiding and protecting him.

Handel was savoring his memories when all at once he noticed a large moustache with a pair of dark eyes just above it staring at him through the steam rising from the bath. As he stared back, the lips beneath the moustache said in French, "Are you not the Celebrated Saxon, Herr George Frideric Handel?"

"I'm what's left of him." Handel replied in French.

"I've heard you play in Rome, Hamburg, London, Oxford."

"And what's your name?" Handel strained his eyes as he peered through the fog-like steam.

"Monsieur Handel, my name is not important. What is important is that I have a message for you."

"A message?"

"Oui. I've always wanted to meet you and speak to you alone. And now, because of God's Providence, I have that chance. You are extremely talented, especially on the organ. Music drips from your fingers. In France we have a saying about talented people. That saying is *noblese oblige*. It means nobility has obligations."

"But I'm not of the nobility. True, my father was a talented surgeon. Still, neither he nor my mother had a drop of royal blood."

"I don't know about your genealogy." The man thoughtfully splashed water over his shoulders. "All I know is that God in His goodness has given you great talent. Since this is the case, you must use that talent for His purpose."

"Am I not doing that?"

"Sometimes, but not always. I've enjoyed your operas. They've entertained me." He sank deep into the water and then used a towel to wipe water out of his eyes. "Monsieur, sometimes people need more than entertainment. I can still remember when I heard your oratorio, *Esther*. That oratorio inspired me. It lifted my spirits at a time when I was discouraged. For weeks I thought about how God used Esther, a Jewish girl, to save her people from the destruction that was being planned by Haman." He submerged himself again in the water. Then he continued, "Monsieur Handel, the world is full of discouragement. Why don't you write something that will inspire human beings to live useful lives?"

While Handel was considering a suitable answer, the slender Frenchman climbed out of the bath, dried himself, and disappeared.

Following another week in the baths, Handel noticed that his right arm was returning to life. Soon he was using it to open and close doors. Ecstatic, he began to massage his fingers. His fingers responded. Within a week they were as nimble as ever. Anxious to learn if he could still play an organ, he stepped into a nearby massive cathedral.

"And who are you?" questioned the organist, a tiny man with enormous glasses.

"I'm a visitor from London."

"The organ is rather famous. Would you like to play it?"

"Thank you." Handel slid onto the bench. He clenched his right hand several times and spread his fingers. Then with a mighty thrust he made the cathedral vibrate with *A Mighty Fortress*. As he played, the organist's mouth sagged. When Handel finished, the elderly man attempted to speak. But no sound came from his lips. On the second try he managed, "A-are y-you the C-celebrated Saxon?"

Handel smiled. "I've been called that by a number of people."

As he headed toward the door, a nun who worked at the baths and who knew his condition, said, "Herr Handel, God has worked a miracle."

"I believe it," replied Handel.

The nun's face grew thoughful. "Could it be that God has worked a special miracle because He has a special purpose?" she asked.

"Perhaps," replied Handel.

18
Messiah

His right arm well, Handel was eager to return to London, compose another opera, and pay his debts. As his ship gently rocked toward England, he gripped the rail and anxiously searched the horizon for his adopted country.

Before he entered his house in Brook Street, he learned that due to the severe illness of Queen Caroline, England was numb. ''No one is interested in music now,'' informed a friend. By inquiry, Handel pieced together the story. While in the new library at St. James' Park, the Queen was stricken by acute abdominal pains. Since no medicine helped, the surgeons operated. And they did so without anesthetic.

A proud England anxiously prayed and waited. For tense days there was no other interest. Church bells summoned the faithful to prayer.

The Prince of Wales was unable to see the Queen. Tense with anger, the King snarled at a servant, ''If the puppy should dare to come, tell him I wonder at his impudence.''

The King lingered at the bedside. He even slept on the floor. Caroline just had to get well! When Dr. Hulst informed the King that his wife would not live, he boxed his ears and summoned the tottering ninety-year-old Dr. Paul Bussiere. Perhaps he could help.

While Queen Caroline fought for life, Handel worked on a new opera. In the midst of his labors, he was confronted by the husband of Anna Strada.

"Herr Handel," said the man, "I've come to collect the money you owe my wife."

"I'm sorry . . . I'll give you a note."

"I'm not interested in a note. My creditors want cash and so do I."

"If you'll wait until my opera is finished—"

"I've waited long enough."

"Be reasonable. The new opera may be a great success. You will be paid."

"All right. I'll wait. But if I'm not paid I'll send you to debtor's prison."

"Debtor's prison?" Handel shuddered.

"Yes, debtor's prison!"

After the angry Italian left, Handel tried to continue the musical score of the new opera. It was impossible. His mind was as blank as a stone. All he could think about was the horror of being locked in debtor's prison. In desperation, he visited the office of an attorney friend. "How bad is it?" he asked.

"Pretty bad," said the attorney. "I'll read a description." He selected a volume from a shelf and read:

> Whether you have wilfully incurred these debts or not, whether you are innocent or guilty, you shall be deprived of pure air; you shall lose your means of subsistence; you shall have no allowance for food; you shall have no bed; you shall have no fire; you shall have to sleep upon the boards unless you can

buy bedding; you shall be forced to horde with a promiscuous crowd unless you can afford to pay high rent for separation; you shall enjoy every possible chance of catching jail fever; smallpox; rheumatism; and every other disease or ailment to which confinement and starvation expose you.

Handel shuddered. "In other words," he said, "debtor's prison is a modern section of hell."

"That's right. And the worst part is that the warden of these prisons get rich from them."

"Then my only alternative is to make my new opera pay," sighed Handel.

The attorney shrugged. "I'm afraid you're right."

Handel was bent over his desk working on his new opera when there was a frantic knock at his door. Cautiously opening it, he faced a messenger in a crimson uniform. "Herr Handel," said the youth, "I have a letter for you from His Majesty. I am to wait until you prepare a reply."

The letter informed Handel that Queen Caroline had passed away on Sunday night, November 20. It instructed him to prepare a funeral anthem to be used at the final services in Westminster Abbey on December 17.

Handel scribbled a quick note expressing his sympathies and indicating that he would write the anthem. A few days later, the Sub-Dean of Westminster selected a passage of Scripture on which the anthem should be composed. This passage fit into the theme Handel had in mind and soon the music was flowing from his pen. The anthem that resulted was declared the greatest funeral anthem ever written.

Handel was proud of the acclaim he received. But that acclaim did not pay his debt to Anna Strada. *What was he to do?* A friend suggested that he put on an organ concert for his own benefit.

"But I can't do dat!" exclaimed Handel.

"Why not?"

"It vud not be right." He shook his head.

"You've helped others."

"Yah, but dat's different."

"Nonsense. Londoners love your music. You would be inspiring them."

So many tickets were sold to Handel's recital that hundreds of extra chairs had to be provided. The next morning the near-bankrupt composer deposited over one thousand pounds in the Bank of England and Anna Strada's husband was paid in full. That payment shifted a staggering load from Handel's shoulders. However, there were many other overdue notes that required payment.

Handel was still haunted by thoughts of debtor's prison. Because of this pressure, he continued to write more and more operas. Some of these were acclaimed by the critics, but few of them enabled him to make payments on his debts. Several even increased his debts.

During this bleak period, newspapers openly accused him of having maggots in his head. Then, while stumbling along in the gutter of despair, Handel met Charles Jennens, the most bizarre gentleman he had ever known.

Jennens had inherited an enormous fortune, and bachelor that he was, he spent it on lavish living. Among other conceits, he was convinced that he was a literary genius. He attempted to revise Shakespeare! Fifteen years younger than Handel, he was overweight and extremely fond of display. Whenever he visited his publisher, he rode in a magnificent coach, drawn by horses wearing elaborate plumes, and with a pair of uniformed slaves riding overhead. Each time he descended from the coach, the slaves were required to advance in front of him and sweep away any debris that might soil their master's shoes.

Charles Jennens called on Handel with a libretto titled *Saul*. "It is based on Israel's first king," exclaimed the playboy in his extravagant manner. "It will make an excellent oratorio."

The city loved *Saul*. But it only played six nights. In desperation Handel produced *Israel in Egypt*. It also was appreciated but not well attended. London had other things to think about. A major concern was Captain Robert Jenkins' ear.

While Jenkins was commanding the *Rebecca* in West Indian waters in 1731, the Spanish boarded it, looted the cargo, and hung Captain Jenkins to a yardarm. When he was nearly dead, they let him down, lopped off his ear with a sword, and tossed it into his face. Then the Spanish captain said, "Take that to England and give it to King George."

Jenkins did what he was told. King George ordered an investigation. When seven years passed without results, Jenkins addressed a parliamentary committee. At the most dramatic part of his speech, he unwrapped the ear, displayed the grisly bit of flesh, lifted his voice and said, "I then commended my soul to God and my life to my country."

Crowds of Londoners began to march while they shouted, "Horns! Horns! War with Spain! Remember Jenkins' Ear! We will have war! Horns! Horns!" Handel watched fanatics thump down the streets, wave banners, and demand war.

England declared war against Spain on October 19, 1739, which pleased the public and stopped the marches. Crowds returned to the music halls. Handel revived *Alexander's Feast*, *Acis and Galatea*, and *Ode for St. Cecilia's Day*. He enjoyed depositing money in the bank.

He was able to reduce his debts. Then the Thames froze.

The Thames had frozen before, but never in memory had it frozen as solidly as this time. The smooth surface introduced a new mania. Fires were built on the ice; beef was barbecued in the center of the river; ice-skating became a passion; shops were opened; refreshments served.

The wealthy enjoyed the river. But the poor endured hard times. Thousands perished. Music halls were forsaken. People stayed at home and warmed themselves by what fires they could afford. Handel advertised that he had warmed his theater. It did no good. He played to nearly empty houses.

Intense cold was not London's only problem. England was at war with Spain. To raise revenue all sorts of taxes were imposed. Since England was already heavily taxed, citizens had a hard time paying them and keeping out of prison. Wigs were taxed and so was the powder to whiten them. There was a tax on windows, salt, receipts, items purchased at auction, marriage certificates, clocks, dogs, watches, horses, tobacco, and other items. Each male servant was taxed, and there were taxes on rents.

Eventually the Thames thawed, and the war ended. But the taste for opera, especially Italian opera, had all but disappeared. Handel was just a memory. Former friends forgot where he lived. His one loyal acquaintance was Sir Hans Sloane, a thrifty man and a collector of priceless books. George Frideric loved him and often walked over to Bloomsbury Square to chat and to view his new books. One day while holding an extremely expensive volume, he carelessly rested a buttered muffin on its cover. A painful silence followed.

Finally, Sir Hans became unglued. Handel

apologized, but his apology was not accepted. The buttered muffin had ruined his welcome. He stepped out onto the street and never returned.

Handel's one comfort in those painful days was worshiping in the house of the Lord. He faithfully attended St. George's, an Anglican church. And he spent many hours each week searching the Bible. To him, Jesus Christ remained a living reality; and, although he lived in an age of loose morals, his conduct was always on a high level.

The months moved slowly by, and Handel sank deeper and deeper into obscurity. He passed the time by studying newspapers and hoping that the mood in London would change in his favor. He was especially interested in the work of Captain Thomas Coram, an American shipbuilder, who had moved to London and become a wealthy merchant. Coram was horrified at the number of discarded children left to die in the streets, alleys, and garbage dumps of London. After years of struggle, he finally received a license to set up the Foundling Hospital. Handel wished he could prosper enough so that he could support it financially.

One afternoon after he read about three infants rescued from doorsteps and another from a heap of ashes, there was a sharp knock at his door. A glance out of the window revealed a gilded carriage drawn by a set of matched horses with bright plumes.

"Herr Handel," said Charles Jennens after he had seated himself in a chair, "I've brought you a new libretto. Look it over and see if you can use it. It will make a wonderful oratorio."

While alone, Handel studied the libretto. He discovered that its title *Messiah* came from the fact that it was the story of Jesus Christ. But instead of using just the Gospels, the author had gone back into the Old Testament and employed prophecies foretelling the coming of Christ. Handel's quick eye noted references from Job, Psalms, Isaiah, Lamentations, Haggai, Zechariah, Malachi, Matthew, Mark, Luke, John, the Epistles of Paul, and Revelation. He especially liked the passage from Revelation 19:6 "Alleluia: for the Lord God omnipotent reigneth." He remembered the time he read it to his father on his deathbed and how his father asked him to read it again and to read it slowly. That distant memory came into sharp focus. Again he saw his father's wasted face, the position of the pictures on the wall, the jug and basin on the corner table, the open Bible. He also became aware of the smell of strong medicine, and the feel of his father's hand as it was growing cold in death. Then he remembered his father's labored comment after he finished slowly rereading the words:

"Those words, my son, are true. God rules. I lived through a part of the Thirty Years' War. I lost my wife and children during the plague, and eight years ago I nearly died. But I believe God rules and God has a purpose in everything. Yes, everything!"

On Saturday, August 22, 1741, Handel seated himself at his desk in a front room of his home on Brook Street. After spreading the libretto a little to his left, he bowed his head and begged the Lord's blessings. Next, he eagerly picked up a stack of blank music sheets and wrote at the top MESSIAH.

The fifty-six-year-old musician stared into space for a moment, chewed the end of his quill, dipped it into the ink, and started to compose. Within minutes music began to leap from him in a living stream. It was hard to keep up with the harmony that stirred in his soul. Hour after hour, day after day, he filled sheet after sheet. In the midst of his writing, a servant placed food on the table. He ignored it. All he could think about was Jesus Christ the Messiah, the fulfillment of prophecy. He finished the first part in seven days. The second part required nine days, and the final part six days. He used another two days to finish the instrumentation. Thus, the oratorio *Messiah* was completed in twenty-four days. This was a miracle of creativity, even for fast-working Handel.

A servant approached Handel just as he was concluding the "Hallelujah Chorus." Tears dripping on his desk, the near-bankrupt composer exclaimed, "I did tink I did see all heaven before me and da great God himself."

Instead of staging his new oratorio immediately, Handel locked it in a drawer. The reason? He had no money to pay musicians, and he felt certain that due to its sacred theme the Bishop of London would stop its production, especially in a normal theater. While he puzzled over what to do, he lingered at his desk composing another oratorio, *Samson*.

The libretto for Samson was written by Newburgh Hamilton. He had based it on John Milton's last masterpiece, "Samson Agonistes." This poem, inspired by Old Testament Samson whose eyes were put out by the Philistines, had been dictated by Milton during his own blindness.

Again, Handel composed quickly. He completed the first part of *Samson* in seven days.

While still working on *Samson*, Handel received an invitation from the Duke of Devonshire, the Lord Lieutenant of Ireland, to visit Dublin and put on some concerts. Since he had no plans for concerts in London, and since this would give him opportunity to produce *Messiah*, he accepted the invitation immediately.

Had God opened a door?

19

Providence

To his amazement, Handel was welcomed to Ireland as a celebrity. *Faulkner's Journal* dubbed him "the celebrated Dr. Handel" and declared that he was "a Gentleman universally known by his excellent Compositions in all kinds of Musick . . ."

That note lifted Handel's spirits higher than they had been for years. Walking on air, he rented a house and prepared his concerts. Joyfully he learned that his first violinist, Matthew Dubourg, and Mrs. Cibber were already there. Mrs.Cibber was not a great singer like Cuzzoni or Anna Strada, but she was an accomplished actress. She had made a name for herself as Polly Peachum in *The Beggar's Opera*. One thing that worried Handel was that she was having trouble with her husband. Sometimes she cried herself to sleep.

Handel's first concert was performed on December 23 in the New Musick Hall in Dublin. For the first time in his life tickets for six nights of organ recitals were sold ahead of time. Handel explained this in a

letter to Charles Jennens: "The Nobility did me the
Honour to make among themselves a Subscription for
6 Nights, which did fill a room of 600 Persons, so that
I needed not sell one single Ticket at the Door."

Faulkner's Journal was ecstatic:

> The Performance was superior to any Thing of the
> Kind in this Kingdom before; and our Nobility and
> Gentry to show their taste for all Kind of Genius,
> expressed their great Satisfaction. . . .

For the first time in years, Handel was prosperous.
Again he was able to enter restaurants and polish off
two meals at a time. Admirers followed him on the
streets, asked for his autograph, peeked through his
windows, and purchased tickets weeks ahead of
performance.

Each week Handel considered producing *Messiah*;
but each week, due to one delay or another, he decided
to feature *Water Music* or *Alexander's Feast* or something
else. Finally as icicles and snow were melting, and
trees were putting out new shoots, *Faulkner's Journal*
and the *Dublin Newsletter* displayed a joint
announcement:

> For Relief of the Prisoners . . . and for the Sup-
> port of Mercer's Hospital in Stephen's Street, and
> of the Charitable Infirmary on the Inns Quay, on
> Monday, the 12th of April, will be performed at the
> Musick Hall in Fishamble Street, Mr. Handel's new
> Grand Oratorio, call'd the *Messiah*, in which the
> Gentlemen of the Choirs of both Cathedrals will
> assist.

Interest in this, the first production of *Messiah*, was
so intense, men were requested to come without
swords and women without hoops. This was so that
seven hundred could be squeezed into a space built
for six hundred.

Because of a request by "several persons of Distinction" the performance was delayed until April 13. It was advertised that the doors would open at "Eleven" and that the oratorio would begin at "Twelve."

Long before noon every space was filled. Sitting at the organ, Handel prayed that his new composition would speak to hearts. From the opening note the audience was motionless. The orchestra was at its best. When the combined choirs sang, the listeners were rapt. Handel needn't have worried about how Mrs. Cibber would be received. When she sang from the depths of her soul, "He was despis-ed—despis-ed and rejected," Doctor Patrick Delany was so overcome he shouted through his tears, "Woman, for this thy sins be forgiven thee." What the star of *The Beggar's Opera* lacked in voice quality was made up by the compassion of her broken heart.

Perhaps because of Providence, the first rehearsal of *Messiah* was on April 8, which, if western calendars are correct, was the anniversary of that Saturday when Jesus was in the tomb. And the first performance was on April 13, the anniversary of those days when Jesus made his first post-Resurrection appearances. Moreover, Jesus was nailed to the cross at noon and *Messiah* began playing at noon. In addition, that performance of *Messiah* was for others, just as the death of Christ was for others.

Box office receipts were four hundred pounds. Handel wondered if this was sufficient to free the debtors from prison and to help the hospitals. It was.

Messiah shook the city. *Faulkner's Journal* made use of superlatives. "The Sublime, the Grand, and the Tender, adapted to the most elevated, majestick and moving words, conspired to transport and charm the ravished Heart and Ear."

Handel realized that it was because he had lifted

up Christ, that many in the audience had been inspired by the old, old story presented in a new way.
Handel departed for London. Would he still be
loathed as an overfed German? Would the public attend his musicals? He bent over his desk in the little
front room on Brook Street where he had composed
Messiah, and worked on *Samson*.

From boyhood he had been intrigued with this
strong man. He admired the way he had ripped down
the gates of Gaza; killed the lion with his bare hands;
finished off a thousand Philistines with a jawbone; and
pulled down the pillars in the temple of Dagon. To
him, the most moving part was when the Philistines
blinded Samson and forced him to walk round and
round turning their heavy flour mill. As he was composing this part, Handel felt so much identification
and was so moved he had to go for a long walk.

From the banks of the Thames, he watched officers
on a foul-smelling slaver force groups of manacled
blacks to continue their daily exercises. Armed with
whips, the guards stood near their captives. Handel
gasped as an unshaven guard cracked a whip over a
woman's head and yelled, "Jump higher, you lazy
n----! We want to sell ya, not feed ya to the sharks."
Fearing he'd lose his breakfast, he walked away.

Handel wandered back to his desk, dipped his pen,
but could not write. The horrors he had just seen
haunted him. Then his mind moved to other horrors:
how King George II and Caroline hated their eldest
son, and how Queen Anne tried to cripple Dissenters
with the *Schism Bill*. Chin resting in his hand, he
thought about how English kings and queens from
Henry VIII on had prided themselves in being
Defenders of the Faith, and yet how most were utterly
corrupt. Staring into space, he realized that the world
is full of evil. What could a mere composer like him
do?

His mind drifted back to his childhood. Memories of Petrina brought a smile. He had learned from that large, grey cat. When a kitten died she grieved. But after a half hour or so she thrust the past behind, returned to the survivors, scrubbed them, and provided their supper. She adopted orphaned kittens and treated them as her own.

Yes, small creatures in the world can do something. Inspired, he told himself: *Through your oratorios, you can present God and his Son Jesus Christ to the world.* Feeling confident again, he reached for his pen.

Before the opening of *Samson*, Handel was so nervous he was unable to eat. He arrived an hour early and was amazed at how rapidly the seats were taken. Swords and hoops were everywhere. By opening time it was standing room only. Many were turned away.

Ah, but what about the second night?

On the second night Handel's eyes popped, for the King, along with several gorgeously dressed women, strode in and packed the royal box. This was amazing, for the libretto had been dedicated to the Prince!

King George's appearance was a signal for crowds of Londoners to attend. Covent Garden was jammed for eight nights in a row.

"Everything seems different," said Handel to his attorney friend. "Why?"

"There are several reasons," replied the man of the law. "Perhaps the most important is that *Samson* is in English. Another is that your triumphs in Dublin have been splashed in London papers. But the main reason is because of Alexander Pope."

"Alexander Pope?" Handel patted his wig.

"Yes, he's just published his complete works. In the fourth book of *The Duncian* he had a few lines about you." The slender man ran his finger across the spines of the Pope books on a shelf just behind his desk and withdrew a slender volume. "Listen, and don't get puffed up. Remember Pope is the greatest living poet." Enunciating carefully, he read:

> Strong in new arms, lo! the giant Handel stands,
> Like bold Briareus, with a hundred hands
> To stir, to rouse, to shake the soul he comes,
> And Jove's own thunders follow Mars' drums.

"Dat is good!" exclaimed Handel. "But I only have two hands. Who is dis Briareus?"

"A hundred-armed giant in mythology. I suppose Pope was referring to the hundred arms in your orchestra."

"Tell me about dis man."

"Being Catholic, he moved a few miles from London to keep from being persecuted by Protestants. Alexander is a tiny shrimp of a man. He's only four and a half feet tall. Looks like a hunchback. But he's the Shakespeare of this age. Everyone quotes him.

"I don't."

"Oh, yes you do. Have you ever said, 'To err is human, to forgive divine' or 'Fools rush in where angels fear to tread'?"

"Of course."

"Well, that's Alexander Pope. To have him write about you is almost as great an honor as being knighted."

That evening as Handel was thinking about Pope's tribute, his mind tumbled back to Aix-la-Chapelle. He especially remembered when the man in the tub next to his said, "God has given you a great talent. You must use it for His purpose."

He also recalled the conversation with the nun after his paralyzed right arm was healed and he played the great organ in the cathedral. She exclaimed, "God has worked a miracle!" Then, as he was leaving, she thoughtfully asked, "Could it be that God has performed this miracle because He has a special purpose?"

Reliving those occasions, Handel was convinced that each part of the drama had been an act of Providence.

With new purpose, he cleared his calendar for the London presentation of the oratorio which he had written in twenty-four days and which he had placed in a drawer while he wrote *Samson*.

As he planned this production of *Messiah*, he knew he would have to avoid the mistake he had made with *Esther*. On that occasion he allowed the clergy to know that he was producing it. They were horrified. Dr. Edmund Gibson, Bishop of London, banned it. Staging a biblical drama in a secular place, he stormed, would be disgraceful.

Knowing that the clergy would be even more horrified if they knew he was planning to produce *Messiah*, Handel advertised it as *A New Oratorio*. Moreover, he made certain that Covent Garden was decorated modestly.

Handel hoped that His Majesty would be present for the opening night. From behind a curtain, he watched as people gathered. Again he was pleased as the crowds poured in. Also he was pleased at the number of hoops and swords that showed up. Then, when the building was nearly filled, he saw the King and watched him take his place along with several ladies in the royal box. This sight speeded his heart. But he was also pleased when he noticed a number of Lutherans, Presbyterians, Quakers, Baptists and nonbelievers. Next he spotted the ambassador from Morocco, a Muslim. Having a Muslim present was especially exciting.

Knowing that this was the first time the story of

Christ had ever been presented in London in a neutral place, Handel silently prayed that the oratorio would accomplish a special purpose. Extremely sensitive to the reaction of an audience, he kept his eyes and ears tuned to each section, especially the royal box. As in Dublin, the listeners became more quiet as the oratorio progressed. When the vise-like intensity tightened until it was almost unbearable, Handel wondered what would happen when the choir came to the "Hallelujah Chorus"—the chorus which had made him exclaim to his servant, "I did tink I did see all heaven before me and da Great God Himself."

Suddenly the moment was at hand. The preceeding soloist had concluded and the great chorus began the hallelujahs. On the third hallelujah, King George II rose to his feet, and he remained standing until the chorus ended. And since the King stood, the entire audience stood. As Handel watched, chills raced down his spine. He was so overwhelmed he was momentarily blinded by his own tears.

Providence had used him. *Messiah* had accomplished its purpose. The King had acknowledged the King of Kings!

Shortly after this first performance, Handel called on Lord Kinnoul. "Heard your oratorio was a great success," remarked the distinguished man. "Several told me they were really entertained."

Handel frowned. "My lord," he replied, "I should be sorry if I only entertained dem; I vanted to make dem better."

Messiah was only featured three times that season. Londoners preferred *Samson*, *Water Music*, and *Alexander's Feast*. But Handel was not discouraged. He had solemn plans for *Messiah*, plans which he hoped would make the world better for generations to come.

20

Encore

Handel was again popular. He paid his debts. Nonetheless, he had enemies, especially among the nobility. Hired vandals demolished his signs, spread false rumors about his character, made disturbances in the midst of his concerts.

In addition, his health wavered. Again, he feared paralysis. His mind wandered. Bonnie Prince Charlie, son of Old Pretender, James, landed in northern Scotland. As he knifed toward London, Highlanders kissed his boots, joined his army. Cities fell. His ragtime army was not well equipped, but morale was high. Each man was convinced the Prince would push King George II from the throne and restore the House of Stuart.

As the Prince advanced, London quaked with fear. No one knew how many secret followers the Prince might have.

Handel read the papers, watched, prayed, inquired, shuddered.

On December 5, 1745, the approaching

Highlanders with their dashing young leader were a mere 125 miles from London. On the sixth, there was a run on the Bank of England. Lines of depositors demanded their savings. Bankers used a clever strategy to keep the banks from collapsing. They gained time by paying in sixpences. The King was so terrified, he had his valuables loaded in a yacht and prepared to leave for Hanover. Newspapers called this day "Black Monday."

But strangely, even when the Prince had London within his grasp, he retreated, and ultimately his army was cut to pieces in Scotland. He fled to France disguised in a woman's clothes.

Relieved, Handel kept writing oratorios on biblical characters. Each season one oratorio followed another. He used such titles as *Saul*, *Susanna*, *Joseph and His Brethren*, *Joshua*, *Solomon*. Also, he began an annual concert, featuring *Messiah*, to benefit the Foundling Hospital.

Handel's box office receipts continued to rise. Money streamed in from other parts of Europe where his operas and oratorios were played in numerous languages. On top of this, he had an honest publisher who issued his old scores in books and paid him royalties. The demands of this publisher kept his aging secretary John Christopher Smith busy making copies for the presses.

Prosperous and homesick for the scenes of his childhood, Handel visited the Continent in 1750. Between The Hague and Haarlem in the Netherlands, his coach overturned. He was severely shaken, but, eager to spend a few days in his homeland, he continued on.

Halle was a disappointment. Old friends were either dead or had moved away. A strange family occupied his old home. The tenants in Zachow's house had never heard of his teacher nor his widow. He visited his parents' graves, sat in the outside vestibule of Our Lady's Church, slipped inside, viewed the organ on which he'd learned to play, and stopped at his favorite restaurant.

After taking a seat at a corner table, an old man with a cane tottered over to him. "Are you George Frideric Handel?" he wheezed.

"I am."

The ragged bundle of wrinkles laughed. "I'm the driver of the coach that took your father to see the Duke at Weissenfels."

Handel's eyes snapped. "You mean the time the wheel came off?"

"Yah. I can still see you as you came puffing through the mud with that little suitcase. You were only seven or eight."

"That trip changed my life. The Duke, God bless him, made Father allow me to take music lessons."

"Then the wheel came off at the right time?" He tapped his only remaining tooth.

"It did."

"For a while I was afraid it wouldn't come off until we were much farther down the road."

"What do you mean?" A strange look crossed Handel's face.

"Oh, nothing. I'm just glad it came off at the right moment."

The pair exchanged anecdotes for a long time. Then the driver said, "Herr Handel, I have bad news."

"Yah?"

"Johann Sebastian Bach passed away on July 28."

Handel stared. For a long moment he remained speechless. Then, shoulders sagging, he dabbed at his eyes. "This *is* bad news. His *St. Matthew Passion* and *St. John Passion* are unsurpassed. I could never equal him. What was he doing before he died?"

"He was organist at St. John's in Leipzig. His last years were pitiful. The English doctor who operated on his eyes was unable to save them. He became totally blind."

"Did they give him a decent funeral?" Handel asked.

The man shrugged. "No. They rang the church bells. The pastor mumbled through a dozen lines of script. That was all. They did honor him by placing his remains in an oak coffin. But they didn't even mark his grave. And they insulted his memory by hiring another organist before he was buried."

Handel wiped his eyes. "Our world is filled with small people," he finally murmured as he shook his head.

On January 21, 1751, Handel began to compose *Jephtha*. The oratorio was based on a libretto supplied by Thomas Morell. The music came easily. But on February 13 he scribbled at the bottom of the page, "Unable to continue because of the weakening of my left eye." Following ten days of rest, he tried again. By the twenty-seventh his eyes were so bad he again had to leave his desk.

Fortunately, his other oratorios continued to play in other parts of Europe. In his bank he desposited royalties from *Esther*, *Alexander's Feast*, *Judas Maccabaeus* and *Belshazzar*. He also received money from other parts of England. Then, when Prince Frederick died on March 20, all places of entertainment were closed.

Taking advantage of the official period of mourning, Handel sought treatment for his eyes. The specialist pierced each eye with needles, and since anesthetics had not been invented, the pain was excruciating. The first two surgeries seemed to help. But there were days when he could not see at all. When periodic darkness came, he reluctantly submitted to

John Taylor, the English quack who had operated on
Bach. The results were disasterous. On January 27,
1753, a London newspaper reported: "Mr. Handel
has at length . . . lost his sight."

But blind though he was, Handel insisted on playing the organ at his oratorios. Each time, at the conclusion, he was led to the front to make his formal
bow and receive the applause. During periods when
he needed rest, he visited Tunbridge Wells south of
London to enjoy the hot baths. While on one of these
trips, he got into an argument with John Christopher
Smith.

The argument increased in violence until both men
were almost shouting at one another. Finally, Smith
became so angry he stomped away and took a coach
to London by himself. Without sight, and thus totally
stranded, Handel was obliged to beg for help. Eventually, a stranger took his hand.

While working with Smith's son, whom he had
employed to copy music, Handel exploded. "Vat your
fadder did to me vas terrible," he all but shouted.
"But he vill pay. Yah, he vill pay. I left him five
hundred pounds in my vill. I vill now change dat."
He laughed with a grim satisfaction. "Now dat money
vill be yours."

"Herr Handel, don't do that. Forgive him. He's
an old man."

Handel snorted. "Me forgive him? Neber! I paid
his vay from Germany. I give him job. Den he leaves
me stranded on da street. Doorknobs vill become
chickens before I forgive him. He's lower den a
snake."

"You must forgive him. Hasn't God forgiven
you?" Smith put an arm around the composer's
shoulders.

Handel was thoughtful. "Dat He has. "But—" He
didn't finish the sentence.

In spite of his quarrel with the elder Smith, Handel allowed him to continue to manage his affairs. And he did a good job.

As the century grew older, Handel became more and more aware that he didn't have long to live. This meant that he must get his affairs in order. Like Bach, he wanted everything to be straight between himself and the Lord. He wanted to be ready for his final summons. On August 6, 1756, he made the first change in his will.

That first change was to restore the elder Smith as a benefactor, and to bequeath him an additional fifteen hundred pounds.

After his seventy-fourth birthday, he realized that the candle of his life was swiftly sputtering toward a close. His appetite was gone. Restaurants didn't interest him. He merely picked at his food. He wasn't interested in current events.

After his Oxford visit, he had become interested in George Whitefield, the Wesley brothers, and their Methodist followers. Their message of assurance was appealing. John Wesley had attended the *Messiah* in Bristol. Handel still remembered Wesley's slender figure as it leaned forward during the choruses. And now that his sun was reddening the horizon, he was delighted that Countess Huntington, the financial power behind Whitefield's Calvinistic Methodists, came to visit him. She wrote: "He is old, and at the end of his long career; yet he is not dismayed at the prospect before him."

Other Methodists also tethered their horses at Brook Street. Each was an inspiration.

Late that spring, Handel seated himself at the organ in Covent Garden during the presentation of *Samson*. He knew every note and every word. As the drama progressed, he enjoyed each incident as if it were

completely new to him. He listened intently as Samson
carried away the gates of Gaza. He smiled as Delilah
sought to discover the source of his strength; and he
became tense when the Philistines burned out his eyes.
When the tenor began to depict the blinded giant
turning the mill, back-grounded by the jeers of the
Philistines, he was barely able to keep his eyes dry.
But he was unable to dam the flood when the soloist
came to the lines:

> Total eclipse, no sun, no moon,
> All darkness in the blaze of noon.

At the end of the oratorio, when the sightless man
was led forward to make his bow, he was greeted by
a thunderous ovation of both cheers and tears.
Londoners sensed that they had witnessed the closing
moments of a great career.

On April 6, Handel was strong enough to return
to Covent Garden and personally direct *Messiah*. After-
ward, while he was preparing to leave, he fainted.
Friends secured a stretcher and rushed him to his
home. When finally he opened his eyes, he had one
wish. "I vant to die on Good Friday in da hope of
rejoining da Good God, my sweet Lord and Saviour,
on da day of His Resurrection."

Friends, lingering in the shadows, exchanged
glances. Palm Sunday was two days away. Would
he last that long? They immediately summoned
Dr. Richard Warren.

The author of *Messiah* slipped in and out of coma
several times. On April 11, the Wednesday of Holy
Week, he rallied long enough to dictate new additions
to his already revised will. Those additions included
an extra year's wage to his maid-servants, a thousand
pounds to impoverished musicians; and from small
to large amounts to others. He bequeathed his wearing

apparel to his servant John de Bourk. He also included an unusual request:

"I hope I have permission of the Dean and Chapter of Westminster to be buried in Westminster Abbey." He then decreed that six hundred pounds from his estate be used to erect a monument in his honor. His purpose may have been to let the world know that he was thankful for what the Lord had done through him. He was still disturbed by Bach's unmarked grave.

On the morning of Good Friday, the dying man assured those at his bedside that he had forgiven everyone. He then waved them farewell. After they were gone, he muttered to a servant, "Don't let dem return. I'm—done—wid—dis—world."

Only Dr. Warren remained.

Handel struggled through the daylight hours of Friday the thirteenth—the seventeenth anniversary of the first Dublin performance of *Messiah*. People didn't know the exact moment of his final call. But Dr. Warren insisted the composer slipped away before midnight. If he was correct, Handel's wish to die on Good Friday was fulfilled.

The funeral was in Westminster Abbey a week later on the twentieth. An estimated three thousand attended.

A marble statue was duly carved by Louis-Francois Roubiliac and placed in the Abbey where it has been seen by multiplied millions. The sculptor made two mistakes: He stated that Handel was born in 1684 when he was born in 1685; and he spelled his middle name Frederick while the preferred English spelling is Frideric. Even so, he was remarkably prophetic in featuring him as the composer of *Messiah* and placing a page from that score in his right hand. He also showed foresight by featuring the page which bears the line, "I know that my Redeemer liveth . . ."

That Roubiliac so featured his subject implies divine direction, for *Messiah* was not unusually popular in the Eighteenth Century. Many clergymen, including John Newton, author of *Amazing Grace*, were against it. They concurred with the Bishop of London that such a sacred subject should not be presented in ordinary music halls. Newton even denounced it through a series of sermons. Nonetheless, *Messiah* continues to enjoy immense popularity the world over, more than fulfilling the mission that Handel envisioned for it.

And this year, as every year, millions will follow the example of King George II, and rise to their feet as choirs begin to sing the "Hallelujah Chorus."

Without a doubt, George Frideric Handel was one of God's composers!

IMPORTANT EVENTS

1715	Handel composes *Water Music* and regains friendship of George I
	September 15, Highlanders take Perth and Dundee in their hope to oust George I and restore the Stuarts to power
	December 22, Old Pretender lands at Peterhead
1716	Old Pretender defeated
	Handel returns to Germany with King George I
1717	Handel moves to Cannons and works with Duke of Chandos
1720	South Sea Bubble bursts
1728	*The Beggar's Opera* conquers London
	Handel visits Italy
1730	Handel's mother dies
1733	Handel and his partner Heidegger go broke
	Handel visits Oxford and refuses honorary degree
	Prince Frederick begins "Opera of Nobility"
1737	Handel suffers stroke at the age of fifty-two
1738	Handel is threatened with debtor's prison
1739	Royal charter of the Foundling Hospital granted
	October 23. War (of Jenkin's Ear) de-declared against Spain
	Winter. Thames freezes and thousands are frozen to death
1741	Handel composes *Messiah*
1742	April 13. *Messiah* presented in Dublin for benefit of three charities

1743	On March 23, *Messiah* is first produced in London. On this occasion King George II stands during the "Hallelujah Chorus"
1745	July 25. Bonnie Prince Charlie invades Scotland and heads toward London. Following his unexpected retreat, he is defeated in Scotland and flees to France disguised in a woman's clothes
1749	Handel presents organ to Foundling Hospital
1750	Johann Sebastian Bach dies
1751	March 20. Prince Frederick dies August 30. Handel finishes writing music for Jephtha
1756	August 6. Handel makes the first changes in his will
1758	Handel continues to present his annual benefit concert of *Messiah* for the Foundling Hospital
1759	April 13. Handel dies on Good Friday April 20. Handel's funeral at Westminster Abbey
1760	George III ascends British throne

BIBLIOGRAPHY

Bauer, Marion and Ethel Peyser, *How Music Grew* (G. P. Putnam's Sons, 1964).

Besant, Sir Walter, *London in the Eighteenth Century* (A. & C. Black, Ltd., 1925).

Burney, Charles, *An Account of the Musical Performances in Westminster Abbey and the Pantheon in Commemoration of Handel* (London: 1810).

Burton, Elizabeth, *The Pageant of Georgian England* (Charles Scribner's Sons, 1967).

Clark, Donald B., *Alexander Pope* (Twayne Publishers, Ltd., 1967).

Clark, John, *George III* (London Book Club Associates, 1972).

Cowles, Virginia, *The Great Swindle* (London: Collins, 1960).

Dean, Winton, *Handel's Oratorios and Masques* (Oxford University Press, 1959).

Dent, Edward J., *Allesandro Scarlatti* (Edward Arnold, Ltd., 1905).

Deutsch, Otto Erich, *Handel, A Documentary Biography* (W. W. Norton, no date is given).

Dowley, Tim , *Bach, His Life and Times* (Midas Books, 1981).

Durant, Will and Ariel, *The Age of Voltaire* (Simon and Schuster, 1965).

Ewen, David, *Encyclopedia of Opera* (Hill and Wang, 1955).

Flower, Sir Newman, *George Frideric Handel, His Personality and His Times* (Houghton Mifflin, 1923).

Gregg, Edward, *Queen Anne* (Routledge & Kegan Paul, 1980).

Knight, Frida, *Beethoven and the Age of Revolution* (International Publishers, 1973).

Long, Paul Henry, *George Frideric Handel* (W. W. Norton, 1960).

Langer, Herbert, *The Thirty Years' War* (Blandford Press, 1978).

Larsen, Jens Peter, *Handel's Messiah* (W. W. Norton, 1957).

Marek, George R., *Beethoven, Biography of a Genius* (Funk and Wagnalls, 1969).

Marples, Morris, *Poor Fred and the Butcher* (Michael Joseph, Ltd., 1970).

Myers, Robert Manson, *Handel's Messiah, A Touchstone of Taste* (MacMillan, 1948).

Ragnhilo, Marie, *George I, Elector and King* (Thomas and Hudson, 1978).

Robertson, Alec and Dennis Stevens (Editors), *The History of Music, Vol. I* (Penguin Books, 1960).

Schweitzer, Albert, *J. S. Bach* (MacMillan, 1905).

Sedgwick, William Kimber, editor, *Lord Hervey's Memoirs* (MacMillan, 1963).

Streatfield, R. A., *Handel* (Da Capo Press, 1964).

Terry, Charles Sanford, *Bach* (Oxford University Press, 1928).

Thomas, Henry and Dana Lee, *Living Biographies of Great Composers* (Garden City, 1940).

Tobin, John, *Handel at Work* (Cassell & Co., Ltd., 1964).

Trench, Charles Chenevix, *George II* (St. Giles House, 1975).

Tschan, Francis J., *History of the Archbishops of Hamburg-Bremen* (Columbia University Press, 1959).

Weinstock, Francis J., *Handel* (Knopf, 1959).

White, Eric and Walter, *A History of English Opera* (Faber and Faber, Ltd., 1983).

Williams, Peter, *The European Organ, 1450-1850* (The Organ Literature Foundation, 1966).

Wiora, Walter, *The Four Ages of Music* (W. W. Norton, 1956).

Wolfe, Don M., *Milton and His England* (Princeton University Press, 1971).

INDEX

SOWERS SERIES

Abigail Adams by Evelyn Witter

Johnny Appleseed by David Collins

George Washington Carver by David Collins

Christopher Columbus by Bennie Rhodes

George Frideric Handel by Charles Ludwig

Mahalia Jackson by Evelyn Witter

Johannes Kepler by John Hudson Tiner

Francis Scott Key by David Collins

Robert E. Lee by Lee Roddy

Abraham Lincoln by David Collins

Samuel F. B. Morse by John Hudson Tiner

Isaac Newton by John Hudson Tiner

Florence Nightingale by David Collins

Samuel Francis Smith by Marguerite Fitch

Billy Sunday by Robert Allen

Teresa of Calcutta by Jeanene Watson

George Washington by Norma Cournow Camp

Susanna Wesley by Charles Ludwig

The Wright Brothers by Charles Ludwig